CHRISTO-PSYCHOLOGY

CHRISTO-PSYCHOLOGY

Morton T. Kelsey

CROSSROAD · NEW YORK

1982

The Crossroad Publishing Company
575 Lexington Avenue, New York, NY 10022

Printed in the United States of America

Library of Congress Cataloging in Publication Data

Kelsey, Morton T.
Christo-psychology.

1. Christianity—Psychology. 2. Jung, C. G. (Carl
Gustav), 1875–1961. 3. Psychoanalysis and religion.
4. Spiritual life—Anglican authors. I. Title.
BR110.K38 1982   201'.9   82-14888
ISBN 0-8245-0506-9

ACKNOWLEDGMENTS

From *Analytical Psychology: Its Theory and Practice,* by C. C. Jung.
Copyright © 1968 by the Heirs of C. G. Jung.
Reprinted by permission of Pantheon Books, A Division of Random House Inc.

To John Whalen,
who knows the patterns of the inner journey
and brought this book to its final form

CONTENTS

INTRODUCTION

I have been on a personal religious quest for over forty years. My wife, Barbara, joined me in this quest some thirty-nine years ago. Our search for fulfillment has taken us down many roads and on some detours. At the start, however, three things were required of us. It was necessary first of all to admit how lousy was the place in which we first found ourselves. Then we had to imagine a goal worth striving for. Last of all, we had to find a way to get from our present place to our destination.

We began to see that salvation consists of a "from what," a "to what," and a "how," and we have come to find that most human beings at times find themselves in the same lousy place we have known. Life often seems to be a blind alley where it is very difficult to find meaning or direction. We turn to the Christian church, which speaks, sometimes glibly, of salvation and transformation, and we are given few specific instructions on how to find our way out. Theological or religious writing often gives us a "from what" and a "to what," but is silent about a "how." If we enlist psychological help we may find that our troubles are eased but we are offered no vision of the transcendent possibilities open to the human soul. Most psychological writing, even the best of it, gives considerable insights into a "from what" and a "how" but shies away from presenting a goal or direction or value for our lives.

For thirty years I have been closely associated with Jungian analysts and had the opportunity of attending the Jung Institute in Zurich and of meeting Dr. Jung. My Jungian friends, many of them of Jewish background, pointed out to me that the Christianity of the early church provided a perspective that encompassed the "from what," the "to what" and the "how." I also discovered that the depth psychology of Jung (known as analytical psychology, in distinction from the psychoanalysis of Freud) offered an understanding and explanation of this way of salvation. Jung's theories offered no obstacles to the realization that salvation comes only through divine grace, which alone brings about the transformation within us. Both my wife and I came to see that we need both the saving power of the Christian God of love and the insights of depth psychology if we are to be able to offer modern men and women the transforming power of the Christian Gospel.

In 1980 Barbara and I were invited to give a series of lectures about our discoveries to members of the School of Spiritual Direction, which was developed by the Pecos Benedictine community under the leadership of Abbot David Geraets. This book is based on a transcript of those lectures and retains much of their informal style and structure. Some of the material in chapters 4 and 5 is drawn from two of my books that are more technical, *Healing and Christianity* and *Encounter with God*. Readers interested in a more formal presentation of my ideas should read those books as well as *The Other Side of Silence, Afterlife, Caring,* and my latest work, *Prophetic Ministry: The Psychology and Spirituality of Pastoral Care.*

Barbara has been working for nearly twenty years with Jung's theory of types and has developed an expertise in methods of assessing personality types. Her lecture on these methods is presented here in chapter 7.

This book is intended to be a very practical and accessible guide to help people who wish to combine the insights of depth psychology with those of vital Christianity. More detailed or technical works on this subject are cited throughout this book for readers who wish further information.

Jung and Christianity

To assess the scope of Jung's relevance to Christian concerns, we shall start by reviewing his life. Jung revised his thinking many times over the fifty years of his career but he seldom stated that he had previously made a mistake and then had come to a new perspective. Therefore, only by the chronology of his writings can we determine his latest and most mature thinking. Toward the end of his life, Jung was most fully developed and most religiously astute.

A second obstacle to reading Jung is his assumption that anyone reading his works will already be familiar with Freud's views. One example of Jung's tacit reliance on Freud's thought is his assumption that we will accept the necessity of a strong reality-oriented ego before we dare to get involved in the inner world. Jung starts with this premise and does not cover material that he thinks Freud has handled adequately. Thus, we need to study Freud to find out what constitutes a strong reality-oriented ego and how it is developed.

The Jungian world view is described in chapter 4 and is compared to the view of classical Christianity. Having established this base we shall then move on to discuss the relationship of psychology and theology. We shall look at the anatomy of the soul and make a study of its depths and varied capacities in chapter 6. This will bring us to a long and crucial discussion of psychological types and the practice of the religious way.

The process of individuation is an essential aspect of Jung's vision of the person and we will look at the process of the soul's growth as reflected in Jung and in Christianity. Three chapters are devoted to the stages of this process: one to confession and abreaction; another to the importance of love, or "transference" (in psychological lingo), and a third on the subject of growth and education in the movement toward integration.

The last three chapters deal with three psychological themes essential for Christian study: Jung's understanding of dreams, which is similar to Christian concepts of revelation; archetypes, and their relation to early Christian and biblical views of spiritual entities, and the practice of Christian meditation, particularly as presented by Ignatius of Loyola, in relation to what Jung calls active imagination.

Throughout this book we shall be demonstrating the relationship between Jung and Christianity and discussing how he helps us understand the religious dimension of life and discern genuine religious experience. While expressing our great debt and gratitude for Jung's contributions to our self-understanding and our religious world view, we will try not to overlook Jung's shortcomings. What we are trying to provide is a Christian psychology, based on the deepest understanding of Jesus Christ and utilizing the carefully developed findings of depth psychology. Jesus knew the human soul and its more-than-physical destiny. Jung has given us an understanding of the depth of Jesus Christ's knowledge of human beings and their spiritual life.

I am indebted to more people that I can mention, but the insights which are presented in this book would have been impossible without the help and friendship of Max Zeller, Hilde Kirsch, and James Kirsch. The interest of the people at St. Luke's Church in Monrovia, California, in these theological and psychological materials was most encouraging. John Sanford and I have worked over many of the formulations presented in these pages. My psychiatrist friend Leo Froke introduced me to many of the works of Freud and other modern psychotherapists. Andrew Canale has also tested and used much of this material in his private practice in Boston. Dr. Douglas Daher, a psychologist working at Stanford University, and George Lough, a psychology professor at Whittier College, have also used many of these ideas and given me feedback about how students have responded to them. John Whalen has helped in many ways in testing the ideas presented here and has helped in editing the material. Many professors and former students at the University of Notre Dame, in addition to those I have mentioned, have helped me clarify many of these points.

For nearly ten years Barbara and I have had a close relationship with the Benedictine Abbey at Pecos. It has been exciting to see many of the ideas and practices that we have mentioned become part of that creative and deeply dedicated community. We probably would not have given the lectures that resulted in this book without the the insistence of my friend the abbot. (My book *Caring* also began as a series of lectures at Pecos.)

I am grateful to Mitchell Hall, who so expeditiously transcribed and edited the tapes. Cindy Wesley turned my final copy into a readable typescript.

My greatest debt of gratitude, however, is to Barbara, who has lived through the birth of these insights and has been a support for four decades. In some ways, this is as much her book as it is mine, and I am happy to include a chapter that presents her study and insights.

Gualala, California
Ascension 1982

CHRISTO-PSYCHOLOGY

Chapter 1

A PERSONAL JOURNEY INTO FAITH

The depth psychology of Carl Gustav Jung has much to offer Christianity. As Christians who are trying to understand and share the message of Jesus Christ, we need to know as much as we can about what the secular psychologists have discovered. But Christianity has much to offer depth psychology, as well: it offers psychological insights as well as meaning. And while Jung is in some ways the most profound and most religious of modern therapists, he is not enough alone.

Because of my extensive involvement with analytical psychology, I am sometimes asked if I am a Jungian. I usually answer, "No, I am a Christian who has found the thinking of Jung helpful in communicating the world view and message of Jesus to seeking, educated, modern men and women." This is an important ministry. The Christian church would not be here today if the early Christians had not brought their message to the educated leaders of the Roman Empire. Jung can help us with the same task in our culture today.

The Journey Begins

I am a member of the Los Angeles Jung Club. At one time a conflict arose among some of the members. We were discussing Christianity and religion and Jung. Some felt that Christ had little to offer. I was greatly encouraged by a very fine analyst who had been trained as a Congregational minister but never had been ordained. He asked the rhetorical question: "Do you know what the best handbook on individuation is?" I thought he would mention one of Jung's works. But instead he said, "The New Testament." Yet most Christians have forgotten how to read and understand the New Testament. Jung opened my eyes to the incredible wisdom of this book and of the one it describes. John Sanford has shown the remarkable psychological insight of Jesus' parables of the kingdom in his book *The Kingdom Within*.

In the excellent documentary film *Face to Face with Dr. Jung*, the interviewer asks the aged Jung, "Do you believe in God?" There is an awkward pause. Then Jung replies, "No. . . . Suddenly I understood that God was, for me at least, one of the most certain and immediate experiences. I do not believe; I know. *I know.*" The implication is that there are some things that are so important that belief is not enough; we need knowledge.

In August 1945, Jung answered a letter from P. W. Martin, who was one of the first religious writers to see the religious significance of the psychiatrist of Zurich. He wrote these words: "You are quite right, the main interest of my work is not concerned with the treatment of neuroses but rather with the approach to the numinous. But the fact is that the approach to the numinous is the real therapy and inasmuch as you attain to numinous experiences you are released from the curse of pathology."[1]

I became involved with Jung's thought through necessity. Throughout my life I had been thoroughly indoctrinated in what I call the "space-time box" theory of the universe, the view that we exist in an exclusively physical universe. My father was a chemist of the nineteenth-century stamp, and a chemical engineer to make it worse. I accepted his view as the only possible one. Nothing in my college or graduate studies challenged this view of reality. I had gone to church, not knowing exactly why. Then through a series of tragedies my life fell apart. I was studying Immanuel Kant and I found myself consumed with agnosticism. Finally I decided I would go to an Episcopal seminary to see if there were any answers there.

The Episcopal Theological School, now the Episcopal Divinity School, was one of the most intellectual in the church. Espousing biblical criticism in the 1880s nearly forced the school out of the Episcopal church. I was there during World War II for two and a half years. The professors were fine and intelligent men who presented a rational understanding of the faith, but in that period I doubt if I ever heard any faculty discussion of prayer or of experiential contact with God. Nor was there a suggestion that the healing ministry and other charismata might have a relevance today. I graduated from the seminary with honors, convinced that there were equally good reasons for not believing in a meaning to the universe as for believing. That was my religious foundation as I went out into the world as a parish priest.

Some years into the ministry I found myself in a dead-end street. I was intellectually burned out. As I got up to preach the Good News, a voice kept whispering in my ear, "But you know you don't really believe any of that claptrap." This is typical of the experience of many graduates of liberal seminaries, as I have learned from lecturing around the world. Among clergy, a nervous breakdown is often a sign of sincerity and psychic integrity: it means they have a conscience and cannot live a lie. They invite hungry people to church and have nothing with which to feed them. The poor minister who has only intellectual arguments and pastoral care soon burns out. When we no longer believe the rational sermons we preach, we often fall into neurosis. Thirty years ago I came to this place of testing and fell into a real neurosis.

One of my closest Jungian friends, James Kirsch, is a Jewish medical doctor. He was born in Guatemala, studied medicine at Heidelberg, went to study with Jung in the 1920s, and stayed on in Switzerland to collaborate with him. He established a medical practice in Germany but left when Hitler rose to power. He went to Israel, then London and New York, and finally settled in Los Angeles. The worst thing he could say about anybody was, "He doesn't even have a neurosis!" Those with no neurosis are dull indeed; nothing can get through to them. Their egos are protected by steel armor under a gray flannel suit.

Acknowledging neurosis was the beginning of life for me, and another example of Jesus' insight that you must lose your life to gain it. I realized painfully that I could not manage my life. I had a horrible and very real dream one night that Dracula was outside my window. I wondered if I should get up and get some garlic and hang it there to ward him off. My outer life, however, was going well. My wife and two children were lovely. The church was doing magnificently. But this outer life had little to do with the problem and when my wife and children took a trip to visit her father, I was left alone to deal with myself and the monsters that are found in all of us.

Fortunately for me, there was a woman in the parish named Dorothy Phillips. She had written a book, together with Sheila Moon and Elizabeth Howes, called *The Choice Is Always Ours,* an anthology comparing depth psychology and the great devotional classics of religions. Being compulsive in my house calling, I visited every parishioner among the 700 families. This landed me on Dorothy Phillips's doorstep. For twenty years, she had been flat on her back with one disease or another and she had written the book in this condition.

Dorothy saw my tension and suggested that I call Max Zeller, an analyst. Tragically, as I looked around I could not find a confidant within the church who knew enough about the human soul to help me (and who would not report me to the bishop). This is a sad commentary on the Christian church. I had to go to a secular Jewish Jungian analyst for soul healing. Max was a man who knew anxiety intimately; he had been imprisoned in a Nazi concentration camp. He taught me that anxiety must be faced directly and talked out. He taught me that God was real and how to pray. He shared his own experience of God's grace and providence in how he got out of the concentration camp and out of Germany. He taught me how to calm myself by breathing. The techniques that he taught me were those which had helped him survive the camps.

Max Zeller taught me how to deal with anxiety and guilt, depression and fear. He listened and never judged, and I began to live again. By the time my wife returned home seven weeks later, I had changed so much she hardly knew me. Before she left she had felt that she was barely holding me together, but now she decided to go into analysis herself in order to relate to her new husband and to understand what had occurred. Between the two of us, we have worked twenty-five years in analysis. We have discovered that if we are to continue to grow we need to keep up informal analysis, which has so much in common with spiritual direction.

What had my analysis or spiritual direction done for me? How had it changed my life?

The Results

I began to establish an inner emotional stability. The fellowship, understanding, openness, and religious experience of my guide helped me cope with previously overpowering moods and fears. I started to use a journal to record my experiences. My book *Adventure Inward* is a record of how I was taught to keep a journal. I began to pray to a real God who cared and responded. It was ironic that as a Christian priest I had to learn to have fellowship with God through the help of a Jewish Jungian analyst. Jesus said on the first Palm Sunday that if the people did not cry out, God would raise people up out of stones to praise him. In some respects, I see Jung and his followers as having being raised up out of stones when the church failed to do its job.

Jung once had extended conversations with Archbishop Temple of the Anglican church, a prayerful man and a fine theologian. Jung pleaded with the archbishop to send a group of Anglican clergy to be trained in analytical psychology. But the archbishop was not convinced of the need. How tragic!

When my emotions started leveling out, creativity blossomed. I could hardly believe the energy, life, and direction that arose within me. Equally surprising, people started to knock on my door, asking, "Will you listen to my problems?" "Will you be my spiritual director?" I had not hung up a sign saying, "I have been in analysis and am available to help." In fact, in my secretary's appointment book I wrote "class in city" when I went to see my analyst. Working with an analyst was not the accepted thing to do thirty years ago. I worried about what the parishioners would think and do if they found out. Later, I finally shared it with them, and found many of them eager to follow the same path.

But they began to knock on my door long before I gave outward indications of the changes occurring within me. When I talked about this with Jung, he said, "Of course, another person's unconscious knows when you are ready to listen." Then he told the story related several times in his *Collected Works:* One day he was traveling in a railroad coach. Seated across from him were total strangers, a general and his aide. Suddenly the general asked Jung, "Do you believe in dreams?" Jung responded, "Well, sort of." The general replied, "Well, I have had this strange dream." He went on to tell Jung the dream and Jung interpreted it. The general stormed out. The aide came back and said, "Did you know the general? You told him what we have been trying to get across to him for the past ten years."

Jung also enabled me to take the New Testament seriously again. He showed me the inadequacy of my blind acceptance of liberal biblical criticism, which is based largely on the assumption that we live in a purely physical universe. He showed me that some of the extraordinary things recorded in the New Testament still occur. As Hilde Kirsch once said to me, "There is no reason that we cannot have religion in the church as well as in the psychologist's office." When one experiences healings taking place in one's life through talking things out, through caring and real praying, one realizes that this can happen in the church, too. It dawned on me that the healing narratives in the New Testament are real. Jung provided me with this dawning light. Jung made me more critical, not less so. I began to question the critical studies of the Bible that viewed these things as merely myths.

Jung's doctoral thesis, his first book, and the first volume of his *Collected Works* deal with tongue speaking, or glossolalia. Similarly, he investigated virtually all of the psychophysical phenomena reported in the New Testament and other writings of the early period when the church was vital and alive. Jung gave me a new way to view reality, a New Testament world view, so that I could look at Scripture through the eyes of Jesus. The early church fathers related experiences of the same "miraculous" occurrences that are found in the New Testament. These first Christians testified that the Holy Spirit transforms people's lives physically, mentally, spiritually, and emotionally. What can happen now in a psychiatrist's office was also possible then. I began to see that the Christian church had transformed people in its early days. I read Saint Anthony of the Desert; Evagrius, a great Christian monk and psychologist of the fourth century; and the great apologists. My eyes had been opened to a wider vision of reality.

One reason that Jung was able to help me perceive and step into the world view of Jesus was that he provided a new vision of the universe. This scheme of things was very old and yet quite new to me and to most of us who have been brought up in the rational materialism of the Western world. Jung was well read in modern philosophy and he offered a sophisticated alternative to the prevailing view. He offered both a philosophical method and an hypothesis about reality in which there is a spiritual dimension to nature as real and as important as the physical dimension. We are able to relate to both realms. In a letter to me Jung wrote: "The real nature of the objects of human experience is still shrouded in darkness. The scientist cannot concede a higher intelligence to theology than to any other branch of human cognition. We know as little of a supreme being as of matter. *The world beyond is a reality,* an experiential fact. We only don't understand it."

When I am lecturing and people find it difficult to believe that an educated modern scientist like Jung could have come to such a conclusion, I console them by telling them that it took nearly ten years of analysis and study before it dawned on me that Jung was proposing the same view as that of Jesus and the early church: we human beings are amphibious creatures and can relate to either realm, or dimension, of reality. This wider understanding transforms our ideas about prayer, the afterlife, the reality of love, ministry, reaching out to the lonely and the dying, and education (especially religious education). I have written books on each of these subjects from this new framework. In some ways, Jung's greatest gift to me was a fresh and new philosophical stance.

The basic reason that Christianity is making so little impact and effecting so few transformations in the Western world is that the materialism of our culture keeps us from taking the message of Christ seriously. An alternative to this materialism must be offered if vital Christianity is to be realized; Jung provides a good foundation for such an alternative.

Some people abandon their intelligence in order to be religious, and espouse an uncritical authoritarianism of one kind or another. But this is dangerous, for the capacity to discern between truth and error may be lost. We may fall prey to demagogues or other idols. We need an intelligent religiosity so that religion does not become an opiate. Jesus came to save us from our sins, lostness, and confusion, not to save us from thinking.

At one point in my ministerial career I wondered about the effectiveness of the church in dealing with people in their suffering and growth.

It was a real burden keeping the institution going, raising money, organizing the parish, providing fellowship. I thought to myself that I might be more effective religiously as an analyst for I had seen results in analysis. I took a three-month sabbatical to attend the Jung Institute in Zurich. Because of a small inheritance that my wife had received it would have been possible for me to have stayed on and completed training as a therapist. But as I went deeper and deeper into myself an image of building Byzantine Greek churches recurred in my dreams. It became apparent that my business was back in the church bringing with me the insights of Christian Greek thought, the insights that Jung had helped me recover. In spite of resistance I returned to the parish ministry for twelve more years.

In the first months after my return, more and more people turned to me for counseling. I realized that we needed a clinic to deal with the needs that were emerging. A parishioner funded the establishment of a Jungian clinic in the church, in which at one time six Jungian therapists worked part-time. Those helped by the program became some of the most loyal members of the parish. Later, Jung asked me how I ever got away with it and told me the story of his relationship with Archbishop Temple.

Answer to Job

Another gift came to me in Jung's response to one of my letters. He affirmed that I was the first clergyman who had taken the time to express appreciation to him about his book *Answer to Job*. He was very gratified, as he considered this one of his most important and most personal religious statements. When I got this gracious note, I asked to meet him. He invited me to come and the visit turned out to be a peak experience for me. He was an unassuming country doctor, very open, very understanding, profoundly wise and caring. A picture of this side of Jung can be found in Aniela Jaffé's little book *From the Life and Times of C. G. Jung*.

What is my critical evaluation of Jung? I feel much like the man who was born blind and then was asked how it was possible that he could see. He could only answer, "I don't know; I was born blind and now I can see." I have a similar gratitude to Jung and his followers for opening my eyes to the power, the liberty, and the value of real religion and of the Christian faith in particular. He was one of the great philosophers of the twentieth century. Although a psychologist of tremendous power, he may be more important as a philosopher and spiritual seeker. He did not have the final word, but he gives us once again a description of reality that contains a spiritual or psychic dimension.

According to Jung, we cannot grow psychologically unless we grow religiously and we cannot attain our spiritual maturity unless we mature psychologically. He makes the supernatural natural, which makes it even more wonderful. Basically Jung is saying that we can keep all of our mental capacities and still be effectively religious and transformed by the living God. Although he did not see his function as prescribing a specific religious way, Jung's task was that of a midwife, to bring people to spiritual birth.

NOTES

1. Gerhard Adler and Aniela Jaffé, eds., *C. G. Jung Letters*, vol. 1 (Princeton: Princeton University Press, 1973), p. 377.

Chapter 2

THE LIFE OF A SEEKER

In describing the nature of prayer and of human growth, I often use the analogy of the growth of a tree. A tiny seed contains within it all the potentialities of the different kinds of cells within the tree, even those of the leaf. Wherever we see greenness, whether in a needle or in a broad leaf, we are observing an atomic reactor. Those green particles of chlorophyll capture the rays of the sun, and they interact with water and carbon dioxide from the air and the earth to create all the constituents of the tree. Only in the last ten years have chemists begun to understand the process of transformation that goes on in every cell of the leaf. The green particles grasp the energy of the sun, release oxygen into the air, and convert sunlight into an energy usable by animals and by human beings. Such complex processes of biochemistry are all contained in one little seed. As we begin to look at the world with wonder, we come to a deeper appreciation of the wisdom and complexity of this universe.

Jung turned this same kind of understanding attention to the human psyche. In order to understand him, we first need to review his life and the development of his thought.

Jung was born in 1875, the son of a Swiss clergyman, and, consequently, poor. As a boy he had to modify his educational aspirations to what the family could afford. At one time he wanted to study archaeology but could not see making a living in that field. I think Jung resented his early poverty, just as my children resented the fact that I was a poor Episcopal priest for twenty years. Only now, years later, are they beginning to overcome that resentment. Most Episcopal ministers do not take a vow of poverty; they just live it. The same was true of Swiss ministers.

Jung was close to his mother. Somebody has said of Jung that he never knew of a person with a worse mother complex, but look what he did with it. The mother complex is something that can be transformed creatively. When we consider the archetypes we shall see that being close to the mother often involves a man in the unconscious. Being close to the father may have a similar effect upon a woman. Once we are involved in the unconscious, we are open to the whole spiritual dimension in a new way. There was no negative implication when Jung said that he had two personalities. With the one he could, even as a child, go off into fantasy; he could remember dreams from three or four years of age. The other personality was practical and oriented to the outer world.

Another factor in Jung's development was his reaction to his father's religiosity. Their personal relationship was satisfactory. But when, as a teenager, Jung asked his father to explain the Trinity, his father did not take him seriously. Jung suspected that his father was unable to answer in a meaningful way and he questioned the authenticity of his father's religion.

One of the tragedies of the Protestant churches in Europe is that almost all of them are supported by the state. There is no better way to destroy religion than to support it through public funds. The Catholic church, because of its closer ties to the Vatican hierarchy, has avoided some of this destructiveness. Official bureaucracy set the tone of Swiss Protestantism. Jung did not experience much power in it, and neither did his patients raised in the same environment. Yet he had an insatiable religious need that drove him to continue seeking wherever a clue might arise. This led him into many religious back alleys. He was both critical of a sterile Christianity and deeply drawn to vital movements in the church. When Jung speaks, we must remember that a clergyman's disillusioned son is expressing his views.

In his late teens Jung read Immanuel Kant's *Critique of Pure Reason*. He was deeply influenced by this work that had influenced the course of Western philosophy. Kant's thinking was to have a great influence on Jung's mature thought. He accepted Kant's idea that we live in a world of phenomena that we can never totally understand.

Another strong influence on Jung was the prevailing orthodoxy in the physical sciences of the late nineteenth century. In those days the scientists really thought they understood matter. The world was composed of ninety-two atoms of different sizes and shapes. These had only been discovered in the late 1800s, so there was still much excitement about the discoveries. These particles were believed to react with one another according to Newton's laws. These patterns of interaction created all physical reality and would be totally understood in time. Added to this view was Darwin's vision of human beings as the fittest survivors of the random combinations of a mechanical selection process. Human beings were thought to be purely physical and mechanical beings, and the medicine of the time treated them accordingly. Such was the dominant world view in which Jung grew up and was educated. Another tragedy of Protestantism is that, for the most part, it capitulated to this point of view. Catholicism was more resistant for many reasons. In Protestantism, God became a theological idea known by inference rather than a reality known by experience.

When I visited with Jung in his study in Küsnach, he told me that he had been almost entirely taken in by the rational materialism of his time, but that somehow he always sensed that it was incorrect. The possibility of something beyond the time-space-energy-mass box was finally revealed to him when a schizophrenic patient somehow perceived a reality deeply hidden in the spiritual world. The schizophrenic asked him to place his hands a certain way and then look at the sun while moving his hands back and forth. "Thus, you see the sun with a phallus hanging from it," said the patient. "This is the source of the wind," he concluded in an awed voice. This patient did not know that the Greek, Hebrew, and Latin words for wind and spirit are the same. Nor did he know that his method for finding where the spirit came from was explicitly delineated in some ancient Mithraic papyruses. Jung later found a translation of these papyruses. This convinced him that there was a psychic reality with which the patient was in touch. This, Jung told me, broke him out of his materialism.

Professionally, Jung first associated with Bleuler in Zurich and developed the word association test. In this test the subject is asked to give his first association to a series of words. With a stopwatch the tester times the responses, which generally require only a few seconds each. Sometimes, though, the subject can give no association for forty seconds or even a minute: the association is unacceptable, and the unconscious blocks it. Jung attributed this blocking to complexes, connections of thought around unconscious ideas over which the subject has little or no conscious knowledge or control. One of the purposes of analysis is to find out why the blocking occurs. For if it happens on a relatively nonstressful word association test, it can also happen when we are taking a final exam, speaking before a group of people, or relating sexually.

Jung and Freud

Jung had read Freud's *Interpretation of Dreams* shortly after it was published in 1900. But Jung reports that he was not experienced enough at the age of twenty-five to appreciate Freud's theories. In 1903 he picked the book up again and saw how the ideas expressed there tied in with his own. He began to support and defend Freud in various psychiatric journals.

Freud received a copy of Jung's book *The Psychology of Dementia Praecox* and invited Jung to come and visit him. Jung's treatment of schizophrenia in this book had met with little sympathy from his colleagues. Freud, however, was deeply impressed. At their first meeting, in February 1907, they talked virtually without interruption for thirteen hours. Two people who had developed their ideas alone now discovered in each other parallel development of ideas.

A powerful relationship developed between the two psychological pioneers. Being fifteen years older than Jung, Freud saw himself as the father figure. For a while, Jung, too, saw Freud as the father he had never known his own to be. Here was a truly interesting, satisfying intellectual relationship with an older man. From 1907 to 1912, they talked in depth about their discoveries and shared their interpretations of each other's dreams.

It is sad to note that a definite break occurred in the formative friendship between the two great men. An authority problem was one factor involved. While Freud felt it appropriate to point out Jung's problems, he did not accept reciprocal critical analysis of his own self-understanding. This difficulty became pronounced when Jung was discussing the discovery in the peat bogs of a corpse that had been preserved there for many thousands of years. Freud felt that Jung's interest in the corpse masked a death wish toward him and, during the discussion, Freud fainted. Jung tried to point out to Freud that such behavior was neurotic, but he encountered a very negative response.

Jung challenged Freud's authority in another way by affirming in addition to the psyche a meaningful reality that is nonphysical and real and capable of influencing our being and action and our world. From the beginning Jung had reservations about the purely sexual nature of the unconscious and felt that Freud was more interested in his system than in truth. Finally Jung decided to publish his findings, even if they were in bold disagreement with Freud's theories.

With the publication of two books that set forth these findings, the break from Freud was complete. The first, a difficult book that Jung ironically called one of the sins of his youth, was originally entitled *The Psychology of the Unconscious* and is now called *Symbols of Transformation*. It is a study of the fantasies of a young woman, in which Jung discovered archetypal symbols and a drive toward healing and wholeness. The second and more readable volume is called *Two Essays in Analytical Psychology*.

The break was not easy for Jung. He lost his father figure and confidant, and was plunged into the unconscious. Professionally he was totally alone, without a peer of equal stature, and working with the primitive and chaotic material from the unconscious. He entered a dark night of the soul and began to deal with his own inner images.

Jung and the Unconscious

Dealing with the spiritual world was dangerous for him. Many people faced with the same material become schizophrenic. But he had a super-human strength of ego and he returned from his inner pilgrimages a changed man. I cannot stress too strongly the danger of going into the unconscious unless it is done within a belief system that provides a saving reality. Jung knew that he had to take this journey if he were to help his patients faced with the same inner struggle. I am quite sure that I might have been destroyed in a similar situation had I failed to find the risen Christ, who picked me up out of the deepest pits, assured me of my value, and set me on the way again.

Jung described the process of entering into the unconscious:

> An incessant stream of fantasies had been released, and I did my best not to lose my head but to find some way to understand these strange things.[1]

Mystics of all religions have engaged in the same journey and have described the same kind of encounters. The shamans of many primitive religions are led through dismemberment and death toward renewal. They understood "these strange things." But Jung had little helpful religious background. He was trained to believe that only the material world was real and now found himself facing a whole new dimension of reality. His encounter was a real act of heroism.

> I stood helpless before an alien world; everything in it seemed difficult and incomprehensible. I was living in a constant state of tension; often I felt as if gigantic blocks of stone were tumbling down upon me. One thunderstorm followed another. My enduring these storms was a question of brute strength. Others had been shattered by them—Nietzsche, Hölderlin, and many others. But there was a demonic strength in me, and from the beginning there was no doubt in my mind that I must find the meaning of what I was experiencing in these fantasies. When I endured these assaults of the unconscious I had an unswerving conviction that I was obeying a higher will and that feeling continued to uphold me until I had mastered the task.

Somehow the Christian religion had gotten into the marrow of his bones, even if it had bypassed his intellect. I believe that his faith helped to save him.

> I was frequently so wrought up that I had to do certain Yoga exercises in order to hold my emotions in check. But since it was my purpose to know what was going on within me, I would do these exercises only until I had calmed myself enough to resume my work with the unconscious. As soon as I had the feeling that I was myself again, I abandoned this restraint upon the emotions and allowed the images and inner voices to speak afresh.

In this passage we see the difference between most Eastern religions, on the one hand, and Jung and experiential, vital Christianity on the other; the Indian practices Yoga in order to obliterate the multitude of psychic images. He simply wants to escape the illusory world. The purpose of Jung and of Christianity is to transform the inner world, and not to retreat from it.

Jung continues:

> To the extent that I managed to translate the emotions into images— that is to say, to find the images which were concealed in the emotions—I was calmed and reassured. Had I left those images hidden in the emotions, I might have been torn to pieces by them. There is a chance that I might have succeeded in splitting them off; but in that case I would inexorably have fallen into a neurosis and so been destroyed by them anyhow. As a result of my experiment I learned how helpful it can be, from a therapeutic point of view, to find the particular images which lie behind emotions.

When I was passing through my own dark night, I came back again to these passages in Jung. They described what I experienced and gave me a method to work on through the darkness. My Christian faith in the resurrected Christ gave me an image to invoke. I have shared these passages and insights with others in the same difficult position and have been told they were as helpful for them as for me.

I would add that these insights can be helpful in Christian spiritual direction. We can see how they differ from the Eastern religious attitudes as popularized in our culture. I have talked with many people who practice transcendental meditation. As the church was offering them little along these lines, we cannot blame them for trying another method. However, the more perceptive among the meditators realized that the techniques they were taught were psychic tranquilizers that enable them temporarily to separate from their problems. I will never forget one person who came to speak to my class, "A Practicum of Religious Experience," at Notre Dame on the subject of transcendental meditation. He was a very confused and neurotic young man but he had learned a method to get through college and survive without having to cope with his problems. He had learned by a sort of self-hypnosis to bypass his immaturity.

Out of Jung's tremendous turmoil, transformation came. He was reading the Book of Isaiah and came upon this passage:

> And a highway shall be there
> and it shall be called the Holy Way;
> the unclean shall not pass over it,
> and fools shall not err therein. . . .
> but the redeemed shall walk there. (Isa. 35:8–9)

The Mature Jung

Suddenly something clicked for Jung; he began to come back together again. But from 1913 to 1921 he wrote no significant major book. He was struggling to find his own base. Then in 1921 he published *Psychological Types*. In this book we can find the germ of practically everything else he subsequently wrote. A new productive period had begun. The dark night of the soul was largely over. He knew that he had not gone through it alone. Something had helped him.

From 1920 to about 1946, articles and books poured from his pen. He traveled widely: to Africa and India, to the Indian pueblos in Arizona and New Mexico. He was interested in verifying in other cultures what he had discovered within himself. He accumulated more and more evidence that we are all in touch with a vast spiritual dimension.

Then World War II broke out and the Nazis dominated Europe. Some people have accused Jung of having had Nazi sympathies and therefore refuse to take him seriously. Quite to the contrary, Jung was working closely with the Swiss secret service. What is considered incriminating evidence was his editing of a journal of the official Nazi-backed psychological organization. In that journal, Freudian theory was dismissed as befitting the Jewish but not the Aryan mentality. A full account of these charges is found in Jaffé's *From the Life and Times of C. G. Jung*. Jung was trying to keep his position in Germany open so he could help the Jewish analysts there. Unfortunately his own shadow came in and he was never able to admit that he was wrong in some of the things he said or wrote during that dismal period.

In 1946 another major change took place in his life. He was walking in the woods. He fell and hurt his foot but did not realize he had broken it. He crawled out of the forest on his hands and knees. It was winter and he might have frozen to death had he remained where he fell. A country doctor set his foot improperly. It had to be rebroken and reset. In the process blood clots were set loose in his blood stream and three pulmonary thromboses resulted. Every breath became painful. His heart was endangered. He was on the verge of death. He experienced a powerful near-death vision which is described in chapter 10 of *Memories, Dreams, Reflections*. If one reads nothing else of Jung this chapter, entitled "Visions," should be read.

From this point on Jung became even more interested in religious phenomena. He wrote a book, *Answer to Job*, as he was recovering from his brush with death. It is his complaint against God. Instead of theology, this book is an expression of active imagination. Jung addresses the God of the Old Testament, who is more justice than mercy, asking why he must suffer like Job. Jung has said that of all he wrote this book he would change the least. He concludes that Jesus is the answer to Job. In Jesus, the evil of the world is carried for us. God in Christ takes the agony and evil of the world upon Himself rather than forcing us to bear it. In the last pages of the book are some of Jung's most profoundly religious insights and conclusions.

In the 1920s Jung came to the view that most neurosis in people over thirty-five is the result of being cut off from that reality of which all the great religions of the world speak. No man or woman, he maintained, can lead a truly adequate life relating only to the material world: we also need to be in contact with the divine reality that is superior to us. One is stupid, dull, or neurotic if not in touch with that reality. In other words, religion is not some perfume we add to an already adequate and well-scrubbed life. It is necessary to an adequate life.

As we look over Jung's life we see that it falls into several quite different segments. The early period from 1900 to 1907, before he met Freud, shows the emerging genius of Jung but is of great interest only to Jungian scholars. During the Freudian phase, from 1907 to 1913, Jung is developing his own distinct point of view which he tried to clarify in the two volumes that mark the break with Freud. Eight years of inner struggle followed. Throughout his great productive period, from 1921 to 1946, he cultivated research in many areas, including religion. From *Answer to Job* until his death, religion was a central concern and for those interested in religion, this final period is most interesting. Yet we cannot understand it without familiarity with and understanding of the preceding periods.

Reading Jung

Jung dictated his autobiography, *Memories, Dreams, Reflections*, to Aniela Jaffé in the last three years of his life. It is a clear and straightforward account of his inner life and thought. It should be the starting point for any reading of Jung as it contains his most mature and most comprehensive statement. His other writings should be read in the light of it. Curiously enough, in his will he stipulated that *Memories, Dreams, Reflections* could never be published as a part of his *Collected Works* as it is too personal and not scientific enough. It was rather a personal confession of his inner spiritual and psychological journey.

An excellent second book is *Analytical Psychology in Theory and Practice,* which was transcribed from a series of lectures he gave in English. It covers much of his general thinking and his theory of typology in simple English. The anthology *Man and His Symbols,* for which Jung wrote the first article, is excellent for showing the significance of the archetypes, especially in the full-color edition. I would then recommend *Modern Man in Search of a Soul,* a general survey of Jung's thought, and finally *Two Essays in Analytical Psychology,* Jung's first clear statement of his differences with Freud and one of the books that made their split inevitable. Thereafter, one may choose any of Jung's works that appeals to one's own interests. Much of his writing, I must warn, involves long and technical descriptions of symbols, of value mainly for professional analysts. Portions of volume 13 of Jung's *Collected Works* are a good example of his technical work.

As to the religious implications of Jung's work, it is better to read the master himself than the Jungians. Many of the professional Jungians do not have an adequate theological understanding. On the other hand, many Christian writers have an inadequate knowledge of Jung and his practice. There are some notable exceptions: John Sanford, Helen Luke, Wallace Clift and Victor White have a keen understanding from both sides. A recent book, *Spiritual Pilgrims,* by John Welch, compares the spiritual journey of Jung with that of Saint Theresa of Avila and displays sensitive understanding of both figures. There are many polemical articles and books that shed little light on the subject.

There is a deep and important interrelationship between Jung's findings and Christian thought and experience. Jung offers no clear description of human destiny and salvation while the church has forgotten how to facilitate experiences which lead us toward that goal.

Jung gives us a view by which we can critique the gifts of the spirit, acknowledge their validity, and evaluate their authenticity. Today, much of the church is split into two factions. The first accepts the gifts of the spirit without evaluation. The second group denies the reality of any divine intrusions into human life. There is a middle ground, but it requires a theory of the nature of the human soul and how it interacts with the physical world, the spiritual dimension, and other human beings. Jung provides just such a theory, one that has been of inestimable benefit to many seekers.

NOTES

1. C. G. Jung, *Memories, Dreams, Reflections* (New York: Pantheon Books, 1963), p. 176f.

Chapter 3

THE IMPORTANCE OF FREUD

Freud wrote with a logical, persuasive lucidity that Jung rarely mastered. I sometimes think Jung did not use this kind of logical clarity because he believed human psychology to be too complex for it. Or perhaps Jung did not have Freud's gift for clear German prose. From the perspective of Jung's theory of personality types, Freud is probably a thinking and judgmental type, while Jung himself is more intuitive and perceptive. For Freud the important thing is the system; for Jung it is the ever new data of the unconscious.

We are so accustomed to modern psychiatric theory and practice that we forget that they are less than a hundred years old. Modern academic psychology began only about 100 years ago with the work of Wilhelm Wundt in Germany; previously it had been part of philosophy and lacked the experimental dimension. Freud and Jung pioneered the more practical field of clinical, or applied, psychology.

Freud looked at the structure of the human mind and formulated a vision that has greatly influenced everything in our society, from drama and literature to psychiatry. But when he began his practice, the mentally ill were merely classified and guarded so they did not hurt themselves; little more was done for them. Mental illness was seen as a family disgrace and being in a mental hospital carried a worse stigma than being in prison.

Before the French Revolution, the mentally ill were simply chained to the walls of the prison. Little change had occurred since biblical times as illustrated in the story of the demoniac who broke his chains but was met by Jesus and healed. Humane treatment of the insane first began in Florence in 1789. Three years later, Quaker William Tuke introduced improved treatment in England. But modern psychiatry was born in France, ironically, during the Reign of Terror, when Pinel took charge of a hospital in Paris and removed all chains. The results were so encouraging he took over another. He was followed by Esquirol, who opened the first psychiatric clinic. Later, Charcot developed the use of hypnotism to reduce neurotic symptoms. It was to Paris that the young Freud came to study under Charcot.

The Problem of Mental Illness

Psychosis and neurosis are quite different.[1] In the former condition, one is out of touch with reality. In the latter, one is in touch with reality but in conflict with it and in tension and anguish. Agnes Sanford once described the distinction in this way: the neurotic says, "Two plus two is four, and I can't stand it!" The psychotic says, "Two plus two makes twenty-two and isn't it wonderful!" Jung and Freud were trying to help people overcome these illnesses that afflict a large portion of our population. They were doctors of the soul and mind.

Psychosis is usually classified in four different categories. The first is manic-depressive psychosis, which involves violent mood swings. In the manic phase, everything seems wonderful. Then follows a depression, in which one feels hopeless, useless, and worthless. This is a serious illness whose symptoms are sometimes alleviated through therapy with lithium carbonate. It probably has both a physiological and a psychological base. The second type of psychosis is simple depression, or involutional melancholia. One can see nothing of value and may even lose the desire and capacity to move. All touch with reality can be lost. In schizophrenia, previously known as dementia praecox, one is caught up in one's own inner world and not related to the outer physical world. The catatonic schizophrenic lies rigidly in a stupor, totally absorbed in the inner world. The fourth category of psychosis is paranoia, characterized by delusions of being persecuted. A friend of mine has been sued by his brother eighty times in the last thirty years. The brother is a typical paranoid.

In neurosis, there is conflict within the personality. It may be expressed in hysteria, which was more common in the past than it is today. For example, a person suddenly loses control over the right arm, or suddenly goes blind. Yet there is nothing physiologically wrong with the arm or eyes. These are psychogenic hysterical symptoms. Compulsive behavior can also be a neurotic manifestation. The compulsive neurotic cannot stop doing something. For example, Lady Macbeth is depicted by Shakespeare as constantly washing her hands. She transfers her guilt feelings to her hands and tries to clean herself symbolically. Overly scrupulous religious people may have a problem with compulsivity. Compulsive working is so common that we refer to the workaholic. Another form of neurosis is anxiety: one is frightened by life, but does not know what one is frightened of. Anxiety covers one's life like a great oppressive fog. In my own dark night I knew deep anxiety. When the phone rang, my reaction was, "Who is after me now?" The anxious person is always on edge waiting for the bolt of lightning to strike. Anxiety is very widespread. In depressive neurosis, one realizes that there is no reason to be depressed but feels as if the ground has been swept away from under one's feet and that one has no meaning or value. Anxiety and depression often go hand in hand.

One of Freud's first works was on hysteria. The etymology of this word is revealing. It is derived from a Greek word meaning womb. According to the theory, a woman's womb became displaced and impaired the function of an arm, eye, or leg. Hence, only women could be hysterics. In his first work, Freud showed conclusively that men could also suffer from hysteria. He demonstrated the removal of hysterical symptoms with hypnotism, but noted that the therapeutic effects were only temporary. The symptoms returned and sometimes worsened. But then Freud discovered that if he talked with a hysterical patient and came to the root of the problem, and if the person gained insight into the problem, the hysteria was often healed. It was often called the talking cure. Later he discovered that dreams can help in the process of self-discovery.

Freud lived in Vienna, where the church maintained strict social controls and sexuality was highly repressed. Sex itself was unmentionable: the empire was shocked when the Crown Prince Rudolf engaged in an illicit affair and then, with his lover, committed suicide. The hunting lodge in which they died was torn down and a chapel raised in its place. The name of this heir apparent to the throne was not even engraved on his tomb. The shock was probably caused as much by the affair as by its tragic end. Such was the extent of sexual repression in Vienna in the 1880s, and most of the people who came to see Freud suffered severely under it. He extrapolated his general theories from these cases. Freud saw a very limited number of patients in his entire career, for his analysis was an hour a day, five days a week.

Freud's Theory

Contrary to his expectations, Freud found that he could not account for all mental symptoms on the basis of physical causes. One of his great contributions to the treatment of mental illness was his hypothesis that in addition to a brain and a conscious attitude, which he called the ego, each person also has an unconscious. The nonphysical contents of the unconscious, such as memories, wishes, and fantasies, could result in physical and mental symptoms. To the materialistic mentality of his day, this was pure heresy. As a result, Freud was never offered a position teaching psychiatry at the University of Vienna and to this day is little remembered in Vienna. What excluded Freud from the professional world of his day was not so much his study of sexuality as it was his suggestion that there is a psychic reality in addition to the physical one. Irving Stone's historical novel *The Passions of the Mind* gives an accurate picture of the intellectual climate of that period and the ridicule that Freud received for suggesting psychic causation, the idea that a nonphysical phenomenon could have an effect on the body.

According to Freud, the ego enables one to manage one's life in relation to the physical world and to other people. In the unconscious, however, there is a pleasure principle that seeks sexual pleasure indiscriminately. It is called the id. An inner censor keeps it constrained and even keeps one from becoming aware of the id because its desires contradict one's ego ideal and it would be intolerable to face such attitudes within oneself.

Even in dreams, the censor scrambles the message of the id's intent. Hence, the manifest dream is different from the latent one. The censor, in other words, is a built-in system of self-deception. It spares us the knowledge that sexually we are animals. With respect to the Oedipus complex, it filters out the recognition that from childhood each of us has sexual desires for the parent of the opposite sex. Without restraint and censorship of the id, civilization would be impossible. According to Freud, civilization, in the last analysis, is neurosis.

How do human beings deal with those negativities within themselves that they do not want to face? Either we introject our negative feelings and become neurotic or else we project what we cannot face in ourselves onto others. This makes for a distorted sense of truth. A congressman who advocates strict moral legislation and is then arrested for soliciting a teen-age boy is a good example of projection. This is typical of the contradictory behavior that results from the inner censorship and projection.

However, Freud could not explain one common human experience through his model. Why do we sometimes have nightmares? If the role of the censor is to keep objectionable material from consciousness, why can it not assure only pleasant dreams? Why can we not be kept blithely unaware of those disturbing psychic contents revealed in nightmares?

In his book *Beyond the Pleasure Principle*, Freud discusses yet another force in the unconscious, namely, a death wish, a desire to return to inorganic matter. The nightmare comes from this aspect of the psyche. His disillusionment with World War I helped Freud to postulate the death wish. He sent all six of his sons to fight in that war for the glory of the Austrian Empire. When the war was over, he realized he had been duped by propaganda. He concluded that there was a destructive, suicidal element in all human beings and in human society. He expresses this conclusion in *Civilization and Its Discontents*.

Freud's thought can easily be diagrammed (see figure 1). The triangle represents the total psyche, conscious and unconscious. The box represents the physical world with its determinisms, which Freud took very seriously. The small triangle stands for the ego, which operates more or less consciously in the outer world of men and women and events. The shaded part of the triangle symbolizes the id with its pleasure drive. The censor stands between id and the ego, filtering out objectionable contents of the id. The death wish is represented by the black squiggle at the lower left of the id. Projection of the contents of the death wish and of the id is indicated by the lines reaching out to people we meet in the world. Transactional analysis uses three of these concepts in simplified form. The censor is the "parent," the id the "child," and the mature ego the "adult."

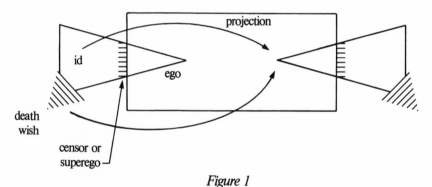

Figure 1

The primary task of all psychoanalysis is to aid in the development of a strong and honest personality. This means the capacity to deal with the tensions of the outer physical world, to practice discipline and self-determination. Some people were so neglected or mistreated in childhood that they never developed such a solid, resilient ego. The analyst must provide reassurance and training to the patient, acting as a parent surrogate who allows the patient to develop a strong ego so that he or she may come to health by dealing maturely and realistically with the outer world, the id, the death wish, and the censor.

Although this theory does not explain all human behavior, it certainly has helped many people to understand themselves better. There is little doubt that many people have been able to deal more effectively with their inner and outer worlds because of their analytical work. Freudian analysis is heroic work, as it requires the discipline to maintain a cold war between the pleasure seeking of the id and an often hostile world. Freud himself is a fine example of what he advocated. In his last years he waged a battle against cancer of the mouth with magnificent courage and little in his system of thought to provide a hope for anything beyond life. Bruno Bettelheim has pointed out the great humanistic spirit in Freud in a recent article entitled "Freud and the Soul."[2] He maintains that most of Freud's followers and translators have allowed their own impersonal and cold scientific attitudes to color their understanding and interpretation of Freud.

Freud and Religion

With the exception of the idea of the death wish, basic Freudian theory can be found in one book, *General Introduction to Psychoanalysis*. It is Freud's summary of his thought, clearly and convincingly written. Anyone who wants to understand Jung will do well first to read this book in order to come to terms with the theoretical base that Jung takes for granted. Jung himself made no such simple, systematic presentation of his thought.

Freud's *Future of an Illusion* is his case against religion. He saw the authoritarian, antisexual Austrian church as a regressive return to the womb, an avoidance of the cold, hard, bitter reality of life. And in many of the people Freud saw, it was exactly that, but his generalizations are based on a small sample. Nonetheless, in spite of its inadequacies and biases, the book has been very influential and a rallying point for people negative toward religion.

The best factual refutation of Freud's thesis on religion is Andrew Greeley's book *The Sociology of the Paranormal*. Greeley conducted a sociological survey to discover the frequency of mystical experiences in the general populace. Built into the survey was an emotional maturity scale. According to Freud, the more mystically inclined people should be the more emotionally immature. Greeley discovered that, in his sample, the exact opposite was the case. The most mature people were the ones reporting mystical experiences. Freud's theory is a theoretical construct that sounds plausible but is unsupported by the facts we have in hand. Anyone who has gone deeply into the inner world knows it is not a pacifying return to the womb. It entails a difficult, painful dark night of the soul and demands transformation after transformation and continual discipline. Freud knew only one small group of people in depth. At best, he merely sounded a warning against the misuse of religion for escapist purposes. But he did not fathom experiential religion.

Freud and Einstein exchanged some fascinating letters. Einstein asked Freud to explain why wars occur. Freud answered that they are a means of projecting the death wish onto others and so avoiding suicide. It was easier to deal with outer hostility than an introjected death wish. According to his final, pessimistic Freudian vision, we are caught amid an ego with no real meaning, an id interested in no more than sexual pleasure, and a death wish. Our job is to conduct a rational cold war so that we do not become neurotic, go on a compulsive binge of destruction, or commit suicide. If this view is accepted it is easy to understand why many are ill at ease with religion. Human reason is the highest development in the universe; reliance on anything else is immature.

Karl Menninger's insightful but depressing book, *Man Against Himself,* discusses the death wish and presents Freud's exchange with Einstein on the subject of war. It also shows that many people are trying to hide from their unconscious darkness in multiple surgeries, psychosomatic illness, neurosis, acting-out behavior, alcoholism and self-mutilation. My students at Notre Dame in a course on death and dying said that this book made an impact because they could see so much of their own attitudes and behavior reflected in it.

How are psychosis and neurosis accounted for in the Freudian model? In psychosis, the ego is inadequate. The ego functions like a stopper in a bottle, keeping the unconscious, animal-like id from emerging and running wild. The psychotic has few restraints. Without a well-developed ego, anything is likely to erupt out of the unconscious in waking life just as it does in dreams. The psychotic is sometimes unable to distinguish between the unconscious inner world and the outer one. In neurosis, however, the ego is intact but in pain and tension trying to keep the nasty contents of the unconscious from emerging. Therefore civilization is created to keep us busy so that we do not have to deal with our inner darkness and chaos.

Jung's Four Major Changes

What does Jung do with this imposing Freudian structure? He makes only four major changes. He never questions the necessity of the ego and its development. He credits Freud with discovering the dynamics of the human personality in the interplay between the conscious and unconscious aspects of the psyche. But Jung disagrees on a crucial point. He sees little necessity or evidence for the censor. Hence, the human psyche is not a system of self-deception. This makes a great difference in the interpreting of dreams. According to Freud, the censor scrambles the dream images and meanings in such a way that we do not have to face our unacceptable wishes, such as the Oedipal urges. For instance, a telephone pole in a dream may be a disguised penis. The task of Freudian dream analysis is to unscramble the dream, to bring out the latent meaning from the manifest dream. If we can, in effect, accept the unsavory tendencies our dreams reveal, then we can get rid of our neurosis and live a rational life. Some people may experience some relief from this sort of treatment. It takes them out of neurotic turmoil and into a less tormented state.

Jung eliminated the censor from his model of the human psyche. Contrary to Freud, Jung said the dream is not trying to scramble any message. Rather it is trying to reveal the contents of the unconscious, but it is using a language that consciousness has forgotten, the language of symbolism. As we learn the meaning of symbols—in the church, in mythology and fairy tales, art, drama, and dreams—we begin to understand the depth of the message that the unconscious is giving us.

Moreover, Jung became certain that the unconscious contained many instincts in addition to sex. Among these are religious drives and a will to power, to mention only two. The repression of one's religious needs might lead to a neurosis, as would the repression of one's sexuality or hostility. There is an instinctual desire on the part of the psyche for adventuring into the spiritual domain as well as for populating the physical one and controlling it.

Jung's book *Psychology and Alchemy* expresses in mature form a third major departure from Freud. Jung worked for many years to develop this formulation. He called attention to a spiritual reality outside of me, yet with a presence in the anteroom of my soul. It is seeking to bring me into wholeness and health, even when I do not know that is what I want or need. Jung called it "the self."

Analysis in Jung's view is not an unscrambling process through which I discover what is within and then, by reason, discipline my action. The analyst is rather like a midwife who removes the obstacles to the operating of the inner healing force within the soul. Jung's concept of the self comes amazingly close to the Christian view of the operation of the Holy Spirit. He affirms that if we look carefully we can observe something like the Holy Spirit. We do not need faith for this, just eyes to see. Jung said that anybody who took the trouble to look through Galileo's telescope could see the moons around Jupiter. Likewise, anybody who takes the trouble to listen to the dreams, fantasies, and religious experiences of people will discover a creative healing reality that alone leads us to wholeness.

In *Psychology and Alchemy* Jung stated his position clearly and forcefully:

The assumption that the human psyche possesses layers that lie *below* consciousness is not likely to arouse serious opposition. But that there could just as well be layers lying *above* consciousness seems to be a surmise which borders on a *crimen laesae majestatis humanae* (high treason against human nature). In my experience the conscious mind can only claim a relatively central position and must put up with the fact that the unconscious psyche transcends and as it were surrounds it on all sides. Unconscious contents connect it *backward* with physiological states on the one hand and archetypal data on the other. But it is extended *forward* by intuitions which are conditioned partly by archetypes and partly by subliminal perceptions depending on the relativity of time and space in the unconscious.[3]

In *Modern Man in Search of a Soul,* Jung wrote:

> During the last thirty years, people from all over the civilized countries of the earth have consulted me. I have treated many hundreds of patients, the larger number being Protestants, a smaller number Jews, and not more than five or six believing Catholics. Among all my patients in the second half of life, that is to say, over thirty-five, there has not been one whose problem in the last resort was not that of finding a religious outlook on life. It is safe to say that every one of them fell ill because he had lost that which the living religions of every age have given to their followers, and none of them has been really healed who did not regain his religious outlook.[4]

In other words, neurosis is a religious matter and the church as well as the psychiatrist should be helping people in neurotic distress. Jung stated that the traditional dogma and practice of the Roman Catholic church created one of the best therapeutic systems ever offered to human beings. It provided for every psychic need: a theory of meaning, a way of salvation, a practice of confession, absolution, and a sacramental life. Jung went on to criticize the concept that human reason is the most developed thing in the universe. Why should we assume that we are the final product, the pinnacle, rather than the handiwork of One far greater than ourselves. There is no logical ground for this assumption. As Jung expressed it:

> It is after all only a tiny fraction of humanity, living mainly on that thickly populated peninsula of Asia which juts out into the Atlantic Ocean and calling themselves "cultured," who, because they lack all contact with nature, have hit upon the idea that religion is a peculiar kind of mental disturbance of undiscoverable purport. Viewed from a safe distance, say from central Tibet or Africa, it would certainly look as if this fraction had projected its own unconscious mental derangement upon nations still possessed of healthy instincts.[5]

So our task is to relate to this reality of the self, or Holy Spirit as it is acknowledged in religious tradition, so it can help us organize our lives toward wholeness and eternity.

A fourth departure from Freud gives us an alternative to the notion of an innate death wish. Just as there is a healing reality that seeks to bring us to wholeness, there is also a destructive force, which would pull us down into disintegration and evil. It could be defined as that reality which tries to make us satisfied with a part instead of the whole, that inferior reality which pretends to be the center of meaning and fulfillment. Evil is seen as a reality both within and beyond the individual psyche. It can only be effectively handled as we turn to the creative center of reality. However, naked evil must be distinguished from our natural shadow, which needs to be faced and integrated.

With these four changes, Jung altered the picture of the human soul dramatically. He accepted the basic ideas of ego and unconscious, of repression and projection. He said little about ego development, assuming his readers would already know about it. According to Jung, we live in both a physical and also a spiritual world. The latter contains all sorts of archetypal realities in addition to both a destructive force and a creative, healing one. Individuation is the process of coming to wholeness. It occurs through our allowing the self, or Holy Spirit, to guide us in that development of the total psyche. It very seldom does this without our cooperation. Some people mistakenly think the Lord, or the Holy Spirit, will run their lives completely. But individuation is a cooperative venture in which the ego must be involved. Rather than being lost, the ego becomes a partner with the divine and is transformed. Jung gave us a new language and a fresh perspective on this eternal partnership.

NOTES

1. The most recent classification of mental illness by the American Psychiatric Association eliminates the word neurosis as a disease category, but it is still a useful concept.

2. *The New Yorker* (1 March 1982), pp. 52ff.

3. C. G. Jung, *Collected Works*, vol. 12 (Princeton: Princeton University Press, 1953), p. 132.

4. C. G. Jung, *Modern Man in Search of a Soul* (New York: Harcourt, Brace, 1933), p. 229.

5. C. G. Jung, *Two Essays in Analytical Psychology* (New York, Meridian Books, 1956), p. 215ff.

Chapter 4

JUNG AND CHRISTIANITY

J ung built upon the work and ideas of those before and around him. He was knowledgeable in all areas of psychology and recognized the necessity of using a wide variety of techniques for the healing of patients. He acknowledged the value of behavioral, behavioristic, and cognitive therapies, and accepted the use of therapeutic drugs. He was critical of these methods (and those of Freud) only when they claimed to be exhaustive accounts of the human psyche and when they neglected important data, such as the data found at the heart of the religious venture since the beginning of human experiences.

To clarify Jung's ideas, figure 2 presents a diagram similar to that of Freud's ideas (see figure 1, page 23), but with important differences sketched in. The triangle in the center represents the human psyche; the whole area of the diagram depicts the experiences that converge upon it, divided into two different kinds of experience by the line down the center. To the right of this line is the world of consciousness and sense experience, experiences of the space-time world, which can be objectively verified. Most of the data accepted by psychology and psychiatry today are limited to experiences of this world. This is true of nearly all academic psychology and of most psychological practitioners, except for a few Freudians and eclectics.[1]

The psyche, however, extends into the world of unconscious experience on the left, with a small section comprised of the personal unconscious, things once known that have been forgotten. The larger section of this unconscious part of the psyche contains all those experiences that have yet to become conscious. Both Freud and Jung have shown that both of these parts of the unconscious psyche have profound effects on human physical and mental health. Impinging upon the psyche are the various archetypes and other autonomous contents of the vast, varied, and seemingly unlimited objective unconscious. Jung called this the psychoid realm. Destructive tendencies are indicated by the dark area below; these impinge upon the psychic depths and spill out into the space-time world.

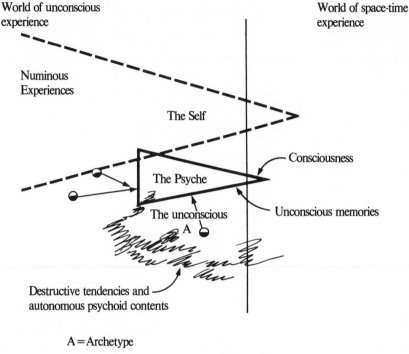

Figure 2

The angle of dotted lines stands for the "advocate" or self (two terms Jung used to denote the positive numinous experience of integration that rescues us from the disintegrating aspects of inner and outer experience). This touches us as with a magic wand. This is an experienced, objective reality, as real as the objects of sense experience, that touches us through the inner, less-known parts of the psyche and can direct our lives and protect us from both inner and outer disaster. It alone gives human beings the power to reach wholeness—it enables the Holy Spirit to become incarnate in our lives. The observable action of this reality paves the way for genuine faith in the actuality of the Holy Spirit and its power. One of the ways we know this saving power is the experience of being picked up and rescued from the tangle of invading negativities into which we sometimes fall.

Jung recognized that his insight was comparable to that expressed in the New Testament. In 1932 he addressed the Alsatian Pastoral Conference in Strasbourg. He asked the clergy to join forces with psychotherapy to meet the great spiritual task of helping men and women discover the reality of this saving power. On the whole, however, the church in Europe and America was not ready to break out of its rationalistic and materialistic shell. Jung and his followers have stood almost alone in supporting the thesis that we can find help from beyond ourselves to bring wholeness and restoration of mind and body.

Only as we reach out for help from beyond ourselves can the opposing forces—those that lead to disintegration and destruction, both personally and socially—be effectively countered with spiritual, psychological, and physical renewal. I have seen remarkable results working with Jung's followers and with his hypothesis about the human personality. In the process I have seen Jung's ideas verified again and again, producing results that cannot be adequately explained on the basis of any other theory I know.

The Model of Christianity

Let us now replace the language of analytical psychology with some familiar Christian language and terminology. Jesus of Nazareth certainly spoke of human beings in relation to two worlds: one of lilies and birds and caring for other human beings, and the other of spiritual dimensions in which one could relate with God and with angelic and demonic realities. He taught that we can and should manage our behavior according to certain conscious goals. He also believed in the existence of nonphysical entities, both positive and negative, that can interact with human beings.

He stated that we have to lose our lives in order to gain them and that we can attain a single eye, implying that there are different levels and depths to the human soul. He stated that our lives only make sense when they are open to God's life and we are living according to God's will. He even told his hearers that we can talk to God in the same familiar language with which a child addresses a caring father. He also taught that the Kingdom of God is at hand and that we can share in it now. We do not have to wait for death or for Judgment Day. However, not everything spiritual is necessarily of the Kingdom: there is also evil that is trying to corrupt us mentally, morally, and physically—evil that he faced on Calvary. There is no question that he believed that the soul, which shares deeply in this physical world and is shaped by it, continues on after death.

The diagram in figure 3 represents the view of Jesus and the early church and is not very different from the sketch of Jung's ideas in figure 2 (see page 30). Again, the model represents our relation as human beings

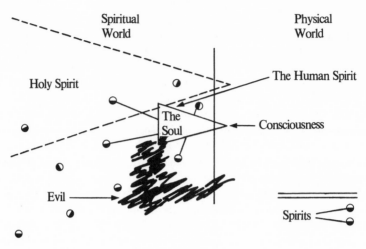

Figure 3

to two worlds of experience—an outer or physical world, and a spiritual one. A dividing line separates the two, but is much wider and fuzzier than a diagram can indicate.

The soul is that reality which contains all of our knowing and willing, all the depths of ourselves, our amazing capacity to remember, our animal instincts that emerge in dreams and fantasies, those parts of ourselves that we have forgotten, and even that part of us which is open to the Holy Spirit; it is the vestibule in which God dwells within each of us. The psalmist does not tell us to ask for the Holy Spirit, but only that it may never be taken from us. The human spirit is that part of the soul touched, redeemed, and transformed by the Spirit.

Obviously, the soul is intimately and integrally connected with the body, which forces it into close connection with the physical world. The body is part of the space-time world. One knows one's body through the five senses, in addition to a proprietary sense by which the body is known directly. Using our intuition, reason, senses, and will we can investigate this world and the very body that makes us part of it. But the soul is not entirely confined to the body. It has a knowing that is more elemental and basic than what we obtain through the five senses, the nervous system, and the brain. Aldous Huxley and others remind us that, very likely, the brain, the sense organs, and the nervous system are given us to narrow the vast range of experience of which we are capable and to focus our attention in order to survive. As all the religions of humankind suggest, we have other capacities of knowing that are found in meditation, mystical experience, and sacramental life.

To most educated people in the Western world the body constitutes the totality of the human being. Even many Thomists maintain that we human beings are a combination of perceptive and rational psychic elements, but that we have no other contact with the spiritual world except when God breaks through to relate directly to us from the great beyond. Most liberal Christian theologians would go along with this idea that leaves out a whole realm of experience of which Jesus spoke and which Jung and his followers have included in their picture of reality.

This picture of reality suggests that freedom is not a purely either/or matter. Rather, it is stretched out on a many-pointed scale. We are partly free and partly determined. The immobilized psychotic has little freedom at all. The saint, at the other extreme, has developed great freedom. Freedom is something we achieve as we grow into wholeness.

The Spiritual World

The question is not whether we human beings want to deal with the spiritual world, any more than it is whether we want to deal with the physical world. In both cases, we have to learn what contents are there and how to find our way among them. In either world, if we try to walk through without looking, we may get by, but the chances are better that we will smash into something or be struck down.

We are immersed in the spiritual world, and when we do not deal with its contents as consciously as possible, these contents deal with us. We may project our apparently positive contents onto others in the cult of romantic love or sentimentality. Often, the hostile elements are projected onto those who seem different and the result is war or racial prejudice, neighborhood bickering or church squabbles, or child abuse within the family. Sometimes the contents of the spiritual world possess us, giving us a messiah complex that carries great, often destructive power.

Sometimes the negative elements seem to turn inward to attack the individual psyche; we are torn with anxiety and depression that seem to leave us powerless and can lead to mental illness or suicide. Many people today simply try to shut off any contact with the world of the soul, with the result that they are plagued by numerous anxieties, compulsions, phobias, and irrationalities that the modern church does not even try to understand, much less treat. When these tensions become great enough— although the person may not even be aware of them—they can break through and be expressed in the body in some form of physical illness. The results of not dealing with the unconscious consciously are numerous and damaging, if not disastrous. Perhaps the only thing more dangerous than dealing with spiritual reality is *not* dealing with it.

One characteristic of demonic psychic content is that it tries to possess the human psyche (in contrast to angelic content, which tries to relate to the psyche). No matter how positive and good a psychic content appears, if it tries to take possession of the personality, its ultimate results are destructive and we are led into further unconsciousness. But that which comes from God brings confrontation, which results in the desire to be instruments of divine love and wholeness. This results in a real problem. Since the angelic and the divine seldom invade us and the demonic does, action is required on our part. We need to be open to the angelic, the Holy Spirit, to the powers of heaven. We need to take active steps to seek the aid they want to give us.

What then are we to do? The first and most important thing is to see that we live in a world that is more than physical. We need to make connection with a religion that deals with this reality and offers a way out. All vital religions of humankind offer a way out. The vital church transforms the high and dangerous voltage of the spiritual domain into a manageable force. There is an increasing awareness in the Western world that our material world alone does not satisfy the soul. We need churches that realize that they have this kind of life and power to give.

There are some of us who are called to make an inner journey of direct confrontation. Sometimes it comes from an urgent religious calling; sometimes it comes out of necessity when we have been plunged into the depths and must find a way out. In both cases, men and women turn inward and face the depths of the spiritual world to which our souls give access. We realize the truth of the dangers and victories so well portrayed in Luther's great hymn:

> And though this world with devils filled,
>   Should threaten to undo us;
> We will not fear, for God hath willed
>   His truth to triumph through us:
> The prince of darkness grim,
> We tremble not for him;
> His rage we can endure,
> For lo! his doom is sure,
>   One little word shall fell him.

An eighth-century hymn ascribed to Saint Andrew of Crete speaks of the same experiential reality:

> Christian, dost thou see them on the holy ground,
> How the powers of darkness rage thy steps around?
> Christian, up and smite them, counting gain but loss,
> In the strength that cometh by the holy cross.

The New Testament is full of these realities, as are the church fathers; and, as Victor White points out in his book *God and the Unconscious,* it makes little difference whether we call them autonomous complexes or demons. The experiential content is the same for one who faces into the depths. There are hundreds of references to these realities in the New Testament, as I have shown in my book *Tongue Speaking.*

As we realize that we are beset by such powers, we soon find that by our own ego power we cannot handle these dark and destructive forces. We also realize that no human being can maintain unfailing protection or defense against them. We who have confronted this kind of darkness must have had some power to help us greater than our own ego or psyche. It is God alone who can come to our aid and is ready to be called upon, as the church has always maintained. Christians are in a very different position from Job in his agony. We have the reality of Jesus Christ, who was the best of human beings and who inspired men and women by his reality to think of him as more than human. This person Jesus met evil on the cross, was apparently defeated by it, and then rose again triumphant, defeating that evil dominion.

When we find ourselves facing evil that we cannot manage by ourselves, we can call upon the Spirit of the risen and victorious Christ. More ready than most of us imagine, this same loving Spirit is waiting at the door of our deepest inner being, gladly enters and lifts us up out of the radical evil over which we have no power, and once we are rescued shows us those aspects that appeared evil to us and that we must try to integrate. In *The Other Side of Silence* I have given some practical suggestions on how we can open ourselves to that saving power.

The journey of encounter should not be made alone. Jung stressed our need for companionship and structure throughout his writings. Several times he suggested that the dogmatic structure of the Catholic church offers potentially the best system of relationship to the unconscious and the spiritual world that human beings have. It offers mediation between humans and the realm of the spiritual, giving protection from the destructive elements and access to the creative, and also provides a mediating priesthood. Since human beings need this inward confrontation to survive but only the strongest personalities can survive it without fellowship and perspective, the church needs to provide the mediation through doctrine and in living practice. This is the reason for its missionary activity. The church has something to give that can be found nowhere else.

Yet many Jews, Protestants, and present-day Catholics have been torn from the systematic fabric of religion and are forced to make their own adaptation to the spiritual world. Jung discovered that many of his patients came to him simply because their lack of religious framework had made them neurotic. In talking with him I learned that he did not get into the area of meaning and religious direction because he wanted to, but because he could find no clergy who knew this realm to whom he could refer patients who needed help along these lines. One of Jung's friends, the Protestant minister Hans Schaer, has described in detail Jung's convictions about the power and vitality of Christianity when it mediates a confrontation with God and gives protection along the way. This book has the somewhat unwieldy title *Religion and the Cure of Souls in Jung's Psychology*.

NOTES

1. Dr. Roger Walsh points out the inadequacy of this framework in the *American Journal of Psychiatry* in an article that appeared in June 1980 entitled "The Consciousness Disciplines and the Behavioral Science: Question of Comparison and Assessment." Walsh holds both an M.D. and another doctorate.

Chapter 5

PSYCHOLOGY AND THEOLOGY:
THE IMPORTANCE OF EXPERIENCE

Agreat gap has been created between theology and contemporary human experience, which psychological observation and analysis tries to bridge. While many theologians have tried to erect a logically certain system for Christianity, human experience does not provide the kind of certainty they seek. Academic Christian thinkers have come to believe that human beings can deal quite adequately with God and evil as intellectual ideas without being touched by them. In contrast to this view is the practical and experiential attitude, which maintains that the ideas are not truly known and understood until they are experienced and affect our lives. According to this latter point of view, the spiritual world must be encountered in personal experience.

From this experiential perspective, a theology that does not spring from direct dealing with spiritual reality is little more than an entertaining intellectual exercise. It costs nothing but some ego strain and rational effort. But psychological theology, theology of experience, leads us into confrontation and encounter with the whole realm of spirit, neutral, demonic, and angelic. Few people come away from this meeting unscathed. We are wounded and can be transformed; we come to know the dark night of the soul.

It is no wonder that intellectual theology is more popular in most Christian circles, particularly academic ones, than the approach of experience. Who wants to be wounded again and again—even if the new wounding brings new transformation and insight? Obviously, only a theology that understands the experience of human brokenness and hurt is able to help those who have been wounded and are seeking help.

No one can be blamed for avoiding the individual, personal, religious encounter, except people who attempt to guide others, either personally or by writing religious and theological books. The average man or woman can find religious development within the church, where the divine encounter is transformed into lower voltage. They can slowly work at bringing their lives into line. This is not an inferior calling, just a different one, as T. S. Eliot shows so well in *The Cocktail Party*.

When theologians, however, fail to make personal, experiential encounters, then the whole of Christendom suffers and the church atrophies. Writing theology without knowing "the dark night of the soul" is like trying to teach organic chemistry without ever having stepped into a laboratory.

Jung has suggested that the outer order of our world would be more peaceful if men and women would direct their aggressiveness inward, and deal with their own shadowy contents. He went on to say:

> Unfortunately, our religious education prevents us from doing this, with its false promises of an immediate peace within. Peace may come in the end, but only when victory and defeat have lost their meaning. What did our Lord mean when he said, "I came not to send peace, but a sword"?[1]

Of course we can also find evidence of God in history and in the physical world. Newton believed that the order he discovered in the universe can heighten our appreciation of God. How much more complex and mysteriously interrelated is the modern world of subatomic particles? One modern theoretical physicist remarked that only a gravitational force of consciousness operating in the world could explain the order in the midst of this complexity. Learning from science and history about this world of experience roots us in the world and gives us respect for facts and experience. A God who is known only by inference might seem in comparison meager fare when we are hungering and thirsting for the bread and water of life. However, when we become unduly concerned with the physical world of experience and neglect our experiences of the numinous spiritual world, we settle for materialism and meaninglessness and often neurosis follows. But if we are concerned only with the spiritual domain and neglect the reality of the physical world we can fall into superstition and fritter away our time in endless astrological computations or metaphysical speculations, and psychosis is just over the horizon. Balance is difficult for us, but our task as Christians is to understand and value both the physical world and the spiritual one. We shortchange ourselves by accepting only one or the other.

Experience and Incarnation

The world view that we have sketched opens up a way for appreciation of the vital experiences of Christianity, the experiences upon which the ideas, doctrines, and dogmas of the church were built. And these experiences are repeatable. Let us look at the fundamental ideas of the church and see how they relate to human experience: the incarnation, the resurrection, the atonement, the Holy Spirit and its gifts, and the sacraments. We shall find that all of these are profoundly related to human experience.

Once we understand that it is natural for the spiritual and the physical worlds to interpenetrate, we are no longer startled or offended by the idea of the incarnation. In a very real sense every person is spirit incarnate. Difficult as this is to describe in terms of rationalistic materialism, data accumulate day by day to show that human beings are just such a hybrid of flesh commingled with what can only be called spirit or soul. If indeed the divine Spirit has a toehold in the corner of our soul, is it hard to believe that this same Spirit can commingle with the entire human soul, as the creeds of the church affirm? Is it then difficult to imagine that the Spirit of God could become incarnate in one human being, first received in the womb of a woman and then born in one human infant? These things are hardly incredible; rather, they show the incarnation to be the ultimate extension of the action of Spirit in human life.

Imagine that in Figure 3 (see page 32), the dotted triangle of Spirit, instead of just touching the human soul, moved down to embrace that soul totally, but then evil was pushed out and it counterattacked. The human Jesus certainly knew the attack of evil. Joseph was tempted to reject his bride and only the dream of an angel brought him around. The Magi were a bit naive and Herod launched a massacre. When Jesus' ministry began, the officials of his own religious faith rejected him. Finally evil, through the high priest and the Roman government, brought the best of people to the cross. And the Evil One watched Jesus hanging on the cross and rejoiced that he had finally succeeded in ridding the world of the son of God.

But Jesus does not stay dead. Unquestionably, this experience is difficult to describe. But we humans have experiences of the beyond sometimes at the edge of death and there are many reports of the deceased returning to those whom they have cared for on earth to give them consolation and support. I have investigated these data thoroughly in my book *Afterlife*. Indeed the evidence is so common that only those deny it who are unable to consider the facts. If this can happen when ordinary people have died or are near death, how much more likely it would be for this person to do so if he actually did bear the very spirit of God in his body.

There is also evidence that several people sometimes experience the same vision at the same time. The resurrection appearances are easily understood as at least a numinous breakthrough of such a collective vision, if we remember that the spiritual world, which expresses itself in visions, is just as real (and perhaps more enduring) as the physical one. This does not, however, eliminate the possibility that an objective spiritual reality gave new form and new splendor to the dead and torn body of Jesus. Those who know anything of the mysterious quality of matter will certainly not dismiss it out of hand. Such experiences of a resurrected body, of sudden appearance and disappearance and passing through doors, are only incomprehensible in terms of nineteenth-century materialistic physics. Just as light is both a particle and a wave, perhaps this resurrected Jesus was both an objective vision and a physical experience.

The apostles who had lived and suffered with this man were awed by what they had met in him. They knew that something quite out of the ordinary had occurred before their eyes. There was an unearthly wholeness and power in this man. Through Jesus they were touched by the numinous, the holy, the transcendent—the same experience they had had in their most profound religious encounters as good Jews. Then, in the resurrection, came the confirmation of their deepest intuitions about Jesus. The man they followed was not conquered by the people under the influence of the Evil One. He had conquered death and evil and they now knew that there was nothing ultimately to fear.

In the ascension, this particular manifestation of matter returned in a blaze of glory to the Creator. This experience should not overwhelm us who understand the moment-by-moment destruction and creation of atoms in a star, and have seen human beings create new atoms and turn carefully selected ones into a blaze of power in the atomic bomb. If human beings can collect just the right particles to do these things, I do not find it hard to believe that God was able to do a somewhat similar thing in the resurrection and ascension of Jesus, rounding out his creativity by offering us salvation and eternal joy.

The Holy Spirit and Its Gifts

After the ascension, the followers of Jesus were given a new awareness of the Spirit. These men and women had lost everything but the hope of new life. As I have written elsewhere:

> The Jews indeed carried a burden, a crushing burden. Their task was to make God's righteousness manifest in their external lives. They car-

ried it through suffering and exile; political subjection only intensified
it. They yearned for some direct manifestation of God. While Jesus was
with the group, he appeared to meet and satisfy their Jewish thirsting.
But after the crucifixion and the ascension they were alone again. The
only stability these men had was to sit still and wait as they had been
told, both by Jesus and a vision; being men and women who had known
suffering and hope, they did just that. They stayed together and prayed,
not knowing what might come. It was then that the experience of glossolalia first occurred. This experience was evidence to them that God's
spirit was with them. It helped give them the conviction which sent
them courageously into a hostile world.[2]

The encounter with the self as described by Jung is just such a central
and vital experience. Again and again he observed that an objective nonphysical reality like this could bring wholeness—indeed, health and harmony—to individuals lives, once people could allow it to operate. If ordinary mortals have experiences of power like this, we would expect it
even more for the followers of Jesus after all that they had experienced
and suffered. When the Spirit did break through, it came not only with
the evidence of tongues, but with the power to heal and to exercise many
other gifts that were passed on to other converts.

These common experiences made the church, the fellowship, necessary. Men and women found that they were more open to the transforming power of the Spirit as they met together with one spirit. Their worship experiences even had the flavor of Pentecost itself, and were anything
but sedate. Out of this common worship grew a fellowship of love and
caring that was the most remarkable feature of the early church. And
nothing attracted and converted pagans more often than the love and caring that they saw among Christians. They exclaimed, "Look how they
love one another." Ecstatic worship, individual experience, a fellowship
of concern reaching out to those in need, the healing ministry—all were
parts of one whole complex.

The experience of being filled with the Holy Spirit is a kind of mysticism usually found only in Western thought. In it the ultimate religious
experience is seen as one which does not annihilate the ego. Christian
thinking, in terms of the schema we have presented, sees the Holy Spirit
covering and filling the psyche, bringing harmony out of the tension of
discordant contents and spirits, integrating much of the unconsciousness
that often appears as evil darkness, and forming a shield against irrecon-
cilable evil. The psyche is brought to an entirely new level of reality. Far
from entering the void of nirvana or losing itself by seeking to be transcended, the ego is transformed. It is made a harmonious part of a total
human psyche, which now has a new center and focus. The old center
and the new remain in relation, a new relationship of wholeness.

This experience is most moving, but our human condition does not allow it to remain fixed. Wholeness is tasted for a moment and then becomes a goal, the end to be sought in life and finally found in the next life. We can even turn our backs completely after such an experience and reject it at any time, because there is no fixed end to this process. It is a *way*, not a safe harbor at the end of a journey.

Whoever enters this way is faced with ever greater consciousness and the task of integrating more and more of our own unconsciousness that so often appears as destructive darkness. Each such experience brings new harmony of purpose, often with a sense of creative peace, and often physical healing because the tension that produces so much disease is relieved. Each experience opens us farther to intrusions of the Spirit in dreams and visions. It also brings greater understanding and compassion for others, changing the destructive critical nature in each of us; we are more kind, or more firm when necessary. In fact the surest way to tell whether the Spirit has had a hand in such an experience is to see whether we have become more forgiving and caring. If not, we may be possessed by some archetypal power, partial and ambivalent, rather than filled with the Spirit of God, of wholeness.

There was nothing far out about this revelation of the Holy Spirit. God had been reaching out to touch men and women through all the ages. Once God had broken through into historical time and space, and meaning had been unveiled, the way was open, and people were in a better position to appreciate the experiences that the divine could give them. Thus the experiences of individuals, shared and tested by the fellowship, gave personal guidance, understanding, and direction to the struggling church. Knowing as they did that God loved us enough to become embodied in the physical world, it was not hard to believe that God would continue to break through to them in visions and dreams, in prophecies and healings. It would have been surprising if this God of love had not.

The early church apparently held little of the idea that human brokenness and sin are so repellent to God that the Father will have nothing to do with us. The apostles told of God touching their lives, not only in clear messages, but also in images on which they had to meditate, as Peter did after his ecstasy in Joppa. The same tradition continued from the accounts of the early saints and martyrs through the ante-Nicene fathers to the doctors of the church.[3] With their understanding that the soul participates in the spiritual world, these men and women did not question the need to listen to these experiences. If God or the Holy Spirit might break through at any time, it was up to the individual to be open to the spiritual world and whatever it brought in dreams and visions, in intuition or spiritual and mental transformation. It was also their job to pass on to others whatever each one was able to receive in understanding and healing experiences.

The Experience of Atonement

There was a real danger in this openness. Being so open to the spiritual world, Christians were more open to evil as well as to the Holy Spirit. Indeed, it was expected that the more they were committed to the Christian community and its life and the greater their influence in the world, the more they would be selected as targets by the Evil One. Christians would be tested again and again. As Tertullian remarked with characteristic exaggeration, the devil was fully known only to Christians. But they also had the *experience* of being able to withstand attack from within and attacks of persecution and torture from outside.

Through the church's fellowship, sacraments, symbols, practices of private prayer and meditation, healing, and exorcism Christians were able to meet evil, much of it incredibly destructive, and not be destroyed. From such experiences the doctrine of the atonement developed. Somehow, through the cross and resurrection, they discovered that the forces of evil had been turned back. In his crucifixion and resurrection Jesus seems to have wrought a change in the objective nature of the spiritual world, and those who were close to him were given protection and saved from evil. At present this was partial, but in the last days his Kingdom would fully come and evil would be cast out.

Nonetheless, we must still confront the question of evil and an Evil One in God's world. Christians have no intellectual answer to the problem of evil. We can give no reason for its existence, but we have a solution that works, one that fits the nature of the beast. This solution is the understanding of the human psyche that we present here. When the power of the Holy Spirit comes into a life, the conflicting forces in the psyche are brought into harmony and wholeness, and the person is transformed morally, psychologically, and physically. We come into harmony with Tao (as the *I Ching* puts it), with the divine stream of things, and so are brought into harmony with God, with the world around us, and with ourselves. This coming to terms with evil cannot be given by a teacher. A teacher can only point the way and help to remove the obstacles. In this, the skilled director of conscience and the psychotherapist have the same role; both must have come to terms with evil themselves. Otherwise they act as the blind leading the blind. When the clergy fully live up to the potential of their role, they are effective as psychological healers, as well as bearers of religious and moral healing.

In terms of the world view we have presented, the atonement is the spiritual result of a victory worked out by Christ, as Spirit, in the physical world, through Jesus as a human being. If, as it appears, the outer actions of ordinary men and women can influence events in the psychic, non-physical world, through active imagination, and can even change both psychic and physical circumstances, then the atonement is the supreme example of such action. What happened in Judea when Pontius Pilate was procurator there, was a spiritual drama made concrete in that time and place, with eternal consequences in a world that is not subject to time and space. Christ's struggle with evil was fought in both the outer and inner worlds, and thus his victory was fixed in the eternal spiritual world.

But this doctrine of the atonement was not conceived on the intellectual level alone. In the early church it was the hypothesis developed to account for the experience of freedom and power men and women knew as they came into the Christian fellowship, often finding themselves no longer subject to moral, mental, and physical illness, to demons, or simply to giving up in the face of persecution. Indeed, as Christians took part in the Eucharist, they found themselves transformed by the Spirit. The living presence of the risen Christ broke through, infusing the bread and wine and the worshipers who gathered to make the sacrifice. This sacrament became one of the best ways in which they could hope to be touched and transformed, and sometimes physically healed, by the Spirit.

Holy Communion and the other sacraments of the church, in the framework of our model, is an event in the space-time world through which we can come into contact, touching and participating, with realities at work in the spiritual world that seek healing and other such effects. As Jung has written in regard to another sacrament:

> Baptism endows the individual with a living soul. I do not mean that the baptismal rite in itself does this, by a unique and magical act. I mean that the idea of baptism lifts man out of his archaic identification with the world and transforms him into a being who stands above it. The fact that mankind has risen to the level of this idea is baptism in the deepest sense, for it means the birth of the spiritual man who transcends nature.[4]

It was just this experience, this sense of transformation, that led to the doctrines surrounding this sacrament and helped to perpetuate it.

In the Communion service the individual participates in the death and resurrection of the Lord. Just as it was believed that the Spirit is carried by our material bodies, and that Christ was incarnate in a human body, so this rite is basically a structured situation in which it is possible for the individual to find contact with realities in the spiritual world that have moved Christians since the first century. Of this Jung has written in

"Transformation Symbolism in the Mass," "If the inner transformation enters more or less completely into consciousness, it becomes one of the vividest and most decisive experiences a man can have of his individual fate."[5] Through the centuries this experience has kept the living mystery of the Mass alive, and from this the church developed its teaching and dogma of the Lord's Supper.

When we consider the possibility that a spiritual world does exist alongside of the physical world, independently and in relationship with it, then the idea of life after death becomes quite natural. There are not only occurrences that men and women have described as coming from beyond the borders of this life (as I have described in *Afterlife*), but the resurrection itself stands for the permanence of the human soul as no other event in history.

When a person is conceived of as a physical structure housing a psyche that is integrated into matter but still able to relate to the independent nonphysical world, then it is not reasonable to insist that the whole psyche—which has already reached out beyond the body—must dissolve with the dissolution of the body. The idea of a destiny beyond this life puts our life in quite a different perspective, giving us a very different picture of how we want to live it. It also has effects on the individual's mental and physical health.

Indeed this quality of victorious joy in a vital Christianity permeates all of the experiences that we have been describing, and it requires a theoretical and doctrinal framework in order to make sense of them. Some aspects of Christian doctrine, like incarnation and Christmas, are easier to absorb than others, like atonement, which requires being rescued from a lostness and woundedness. Psychological insight can help us understand and move through these experiences to transformation.

NOTES

1. C. G. Jung, *Collected Works*, 10:224.

2. *Tongue Speaking: The History and Meaning of Charismatic Experience* (New York: Crossroads, 1981), pp. 18f.

3. In my book *God, Dreams and Revelation*, I have presented in chapters 4, 5, and 6 a large sampling of this material from the New Testament, the fathers, and doctors of the church.

4. C. G. Jung, *Collected Works*, 10:67.

5. *Papers from the Eranos Yearbooks*, vol. 2, *The Mysteries* (New York: Pantheon, 1955), p. 336.

Chapter 6

THE SOUL AND ITS CAPACITIES

It is difficult for us living in a predominantly materialistic culture to understand that Jung and the church are really affirming the substantial reality of a spiritual world. When I lecture, people often find it hard to believe that I am proposing the existence of another dimension of reality that is available for experience and important for psychological and spiritual health. I usually tell them that I understand their bewilderment. It took me ten years of analysis to be freed from my materialistic prejudices. How can I expect them to come to any depth of understanding in six or seven lectures?

I have found that people under thirty are much more open to this view, as are those who have experience in theoretical physics and those from third world or oriental countries who have never been brainwashed by the Western view. Those most difficult to reach are behavioristic psychologists and most theologians; the more degrees they have the more resistant they are to the idea. The Western educational system can be a virulent form of brainwashing that actually keeps us from looking at the facts which do not fit, as T. S. Kuhn observed in his ground-breaking book, *The Structure of Scientific Revolutions*.

We have painted in large brush strokes a world view in which the soul, or psyche, is a bridge between two worlds. It is now time for us to take a closer look at the human psyche and its capacities. Again, a diagram will be helpful, as long as we realize that it is merely a map depicting levels and capacities of the soul.

The part of the psyche that juts out into the physical world through the body has been studied a great deal in recent years. The brain, through which the psyche usually expresses itself, is incredibly complex. We are learning more about it all the time. We have recently discovered that the body produces substances that are more powerful than any drug and that can kill pain more effectively than any opiate. Some of these are triggered by the attitude of faith of the individual.

Behaviorists have studied the effects of conditioning on what we do and think; they show how much we are shaped by our environment. We learn our very language by our interactions with other human beings. Totally isolated individuals hardly become human at all; they are like seeds that have never had an opportunity to germinate and grow. Our developed consciousness with its ability to deal with the world is in part due to the experiences we had as children. The will, or self-determination, that enables us to work toward goals is given partly by the total environment and partly by the nature and structure of the soul. The first thing that the psychologist or educator or adviser, religious or secular, wishes to do is to provide a climate of relationship that releases people to develop conscious strength of will and ego to enable budding personalities to bloom or blighted personalities to revive. The most important factor in this development is a caring and concerned environment.

Those who would help others towards spiritual growth need to provide this kind of relationship and this is very demanding, as I have shown in my book *Caring*. Few of us even begin to grow into our human *or* spiritual potential until we have found a relationship in which we are given love that has no strings attached. We continue on this road of growth as *we become* persons who can give that kind of unconditional love. If, indeed, the center of the universe is characterized by such love, this makes sense. As we love and are loved, we step into the pulse of the very nature of God. This is *the* healing factor, the unrecognized and neglected variable, that is crucial in our preparation and our journey upon the road to wholeness. In this matter Jesus, the church at its most vital, and the best of modern clinical psychology are saying precisely the same thing.

Another element in the makeup of the human psyche is memory, which makes learning and humanness possible. Memory is an amazing and mysterious faculty. Just how I can recall (or not recall) the words that I wish to write next is still shrouded in the unknown. People with brains that have deteriorated because of atrophy of the blood vessels may still remember the past with clarity. Tonight I may go to sleep and dream of a person or scene I have not seen for fifty or sixty years and reproduce it in perfect detail. Experiments with rats have shown that animals with nearly all of the brain tissue removed can still remember mazes they have learned, even though they cannot learn new ones. Some scientists are speculating that memory may not be stored in the physical brain, but in a nonphysical part of the psyche.

Things that I do not wish to remember because they conflict with my ideas about myself are repressed and become part of the personal uncon-

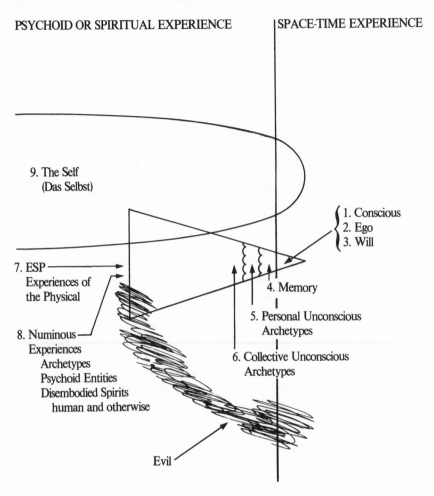

PSYCHOID OR SPIRITUAL EXPERIENCE　　　SPACE-TIME EXPERIENCE

9. The Self
(Das Selbst)

1. Conscious
2. Ego
3. Will

7. ESP
Experiences of
the Physical

4. Memory

5. Personal Unconscious
Archetypes

8. Numinous
Experiences
Archetypes
Psychoid Entities
Disembodied Spirits
human and otherwise

6. Collective Unconscious
Archetypes

Evil

Figure 4

scious. For example, a student once came to see me for help because he was failing in college. He presented a striking example of the action of the personal unconscious. For several semesters he had come down with pneumonia just at exam time. We talked and I asked him if he was aware of anything bothering him. He knew of nothing. For five or six weeks we made no progress. Suddenly in one of our sessions together it was as if a light had turnéd on. He remembered that in his first year of college he and his roommate were involved homosexually on almost a daily basis. It was during this period that his first bout with pneumonia occurred, but at the time he did not see the connection and had totally forgotten about his involvement and was ignorant of the guilt that he was feeling. I had asked him if he had had any such involvement or relationship and he had told me that he had not. But what had been buried in the unconscious did not leave him alone. That which he could not look at within rotted and was converted into physical symptoms. The story had a happy ending. Once he let out his story and began to deal with this whole complex, he had no recurrence of pneumonia. He finished college, went on to professional school, married, and had children.

If we would help another on the inner road, roadblocks such as this must be removed. If people are to be helped in dealing with such hidden material, they must be provided with an atmosphere of unconditional acceptance. When a caring listener can accept contents that have been unacceptable to us, we can begin to accept them ourselves. Freud was one of the first to explain the dynamics of repression and offer a method by which it could be healed. As clergy or lay counselors—or as Christian friends wishing to help people through this kind of problem—we must put off our judgmental attitudes. Again, mature love is the unconditional answer.

Jung knew well the importance of the personal unconscious in causing psychic conflicts, but Freud dealt with the subject with such adequacy that Jung found it unnecessary to go over the same territory. However, he made a discovery dealing with the psyche in therapy. He found universal contents within the dreams and fantasies of his patients; he called them archetypes, the imprint of a "type," or form, that was not derived from historical experience. Here were "innate" forms ready to spring to life in symbols and images; they were universal patterns of reality within the very structure and nature of the psyche. Sometimes I see them as organs for perception of nonphysical reality, similar to the five senses. It is interesting that Freud came to similar ideas after he and Jung had broken with one another.

In Freud these contents are seen merely as part of the psyche. Jung's thought is complicated by the fact that he sees a world of reality external to the psyche and independent of it. And when he refers to archetypes Jung is never quite clear as to whether he is designating something purely within the individual psyche or something beyond it that impinges upon the inner archetype.

Jung came to this formulation largely to account for the dream and fantasy material that could be accounted for in no other way. He also began to study the texts of ancient and medieval alchemy and realized that the processes and images described there were similar to those of his patients. He came to believe that much of the mysterious part of alchemy was a projection onto matter. The alchemists projected their process of coming to psychic wholeness onto the material things with which they were working. I will never forget the interest of my analyst when I told him of a dream of an emerald table inscribed in a script I did not know. He picked up a book on alchemy and showed me a picture of such a table, which was a common idea of the alchemists. Needless to say, I had read no alchemy.

In my book *Discernment,* I tell the story of an exercise in active imagination that I did some years ago and that revealed to me some of the dominant archetypes within me. It came at the end of a six-month sabbatical leave. We went on a long freighter trip and then traveled across Australia and New Zealand. My preoccupation with the outer world was almost entirely eliminated and many things within me emerged of which I had not been aware. One of the reasons that so many of us fear this kind of quiet is that we must then deal with ourselves. During those months I realized how much turmoil and turbulence were seething within me and I dealt with what I found within from week to week. While in Switzerland toward the end of the trip I became quiet and turned inward and a powerful fantasy presented itself.

I found myself in a little cabin on the top of a cliff overlooking the ocean. It was a stormy night. There was a knock on the door. One by one, nine characters came to the door and entered. They were nine archetypal aspects of my psyche, nine that were universal and outside of me as well. The first two were a mother and child. Then in succession and with a dramatic play among them came a Mercury-like youth, a Venus-like maiden, and then a soldier-like Mars, the god of war. Then came an imperious Jupiter figure, then a professor for whom there is no mythological equivalent, then a fool in medieval motley of purple and green. Finally Vulcan, the god of the forge, came stumbling in with his feet on backwards. This was quite a menagerie. I soon realized that I could not manage all of these powerful characters myself. I needed help and I called on the Christ, the symbol of wholeness and integration. I realized more poignantly than ever that polytheistic mythology is really describing a reality within me and beyond me, something that must be regulated.

Each of these figures is valuable as an aspect of myself and is needed as a part of my psychic wholeness. The child gives me a sense of wonder and openness. From the mother I derive the ability to nurture and the quality of earthiness. The youth contributes vitality, imagination, and creativity. The maiden gives a sense of beauty and sensitivity and opens me to the whole realm of the unconscious. Without the assertiveness of the Mars within me I can be overcome by powers outside of me and within me; I need his strength to demand my place in the sun, to protect me as I work on my own development. Jupiter enables me to give direction to the rest of me and take hold of situations in the outer world. The professor keeps the ideas flowing and helps me write books. The fool gives me a sense of humor, without which I am surely lost. The blacksmith is the agent of practicality.

And yet when any one of these figures tries to take over my psyche and push out or take control of the other inner powers, the results are disastrous. The nurturing mother can turn into the all-possessing and devouring goddess. The child who is not protected can become weak and cowardly, afraid to go out into the world. The youth has an irresponsible side; he can become meaninglessly destructive and cruel. The maiden can become seductive and lead one into hell. And we who have lived through two world wars and a dozen minor ones, need not be reminded of the havoc and annihilation that Mars can cause. Jupiter can become the slave trader, wishing to own by force and power. It was the professor who led me into my dead-end street in the first place by telling me that reason alone was important. The fool can playfully touch off a bomb without thinking. And the blacksmith can fashion instruments of torture and of war.

I cannot eliminate any of these archetypes from my psyche without doing irretrievable damage to myself. Rather, I need to bring all of these parts of me together to the self, the organizing center, the risen Christ, so that each may play its proper role and I can continue on the way to wholeness and be prepared for life within the Kingdom of God. I do not have the power to do this for myself. The archetypes are such powerful centers of energy that I must have help in handling them.

Different people have different configurations of archetypes within them. There are few more creative tasks than facing our inner depths so that we can inhibit the demonic aspects of each of our inner figures and facilitate the expression of their creative sides. There are some ministers and religious advisers, particularly among the more enthusiastic and rigid religious groups, who would have us try to eliminate some of these archetypal aspects of our lives—our sexuality or our assertiveness or our anger—rather than helping us integrate them. The results of such an approach are crippling.

It is difficult to share with others our personal failures and mistakes that are so painful they have been forgotten. How much more difficult is it to allow another to see these elements of inhuman destructiveness or lust that bubble up out of our inner witches' brew? Only where there is unconditional caring and love are we able to share this level of ourselves and so learn to deal creatively with these elements within us.

At one meeting with Hilde Kirsch she described the monstrous examination through which the Nazi guards put her as she was leaving Germany for Switzerland. I was horrified, and even more horrified when I realized that I could have been one of those Nazi guards and told her so. She quietly replied, "No, Morton, only a part of you could have been." If we would accompany another on this venture of inner discovery and transformation, we must know ourselves so well that we are shocked at nothing and can stand by with love and support with those who are entering the inner swamp. I cannot bring these individual aspects of the collective unconscious to Christ to be put into proper perspective unless I know what they are. This means that I must listen to the depths of myself and I need companionship and caring so that I do not despair at what I find within.

The Numinous

Jung points out that we are able to perceive the physical world by means other than the five senses. This brings us to areas 7, 8, and 9 of the diagram in figure 4 (see page 48).

Extrasensory perception, or ESP, is becoming more accepted as a subject of serious study, in spite of the prejudice which this subject has aroused in the psychological community. Stanley Krippner in his book *Song of the Siren* reports that he was told that he would never get his doctor's degree in psychology unless he abandoned his interest in ESP research. Jung was much interested in this field; it confirmed his own clinical experiences that people did perceive *physical* reality by other methods than through the five senses. I have examined these data in my book *The Christian and the Supernatural.* Much of Christian tradition (including the Bible) affirms that our souls have this capacity.

Once it is established that we can have verifiable experiences through means other than sense experience, it becomes unreasonable to doubt that we can have contact with disembodied psychic entities. Jung believed that we could be in touch through this nonsensory knowing with a vast variety of psychic contents.[1]

If, indeed, we humans have such capacities but fail to investigate them, we are selling ourselves short. Likewise, if we think such ideas are silly, people will not share them with us when they have these experiences and we can give them no guidance in them. And if there is any area in which human beings need advice, guidance, and spiritual direction it is in dealing with this whole area of experience. People can get carried away by a fascination with these things unless they can share them with those who know this reality and realize that it needs to be carefully assessed and discerned.

Evil and Shadow

And this brings us to the psychological perspective on evil. Genuine evil is that which seeks to keep one disunified and at war within oneself by letting one archetype within control the whole. Evil is the disintegrative spirit or force within the universe, as opposed to the Holy Spirit, or self, which is trying to bring harmony and wholeness through love and caring. The archetypes are morally neutral, capable of being used either creatively or destructively, for good or evil.

One of Jung's important contributions to the understanding of the human soul and its moral dilemmas is his observation that any natural part of us that is rejected turns negative. That part is like a child who has been ignored and becomes a terror, largely to gain attention. The obnoxious child, driven by a need to relate, prefers negative attention to none at all. How often we need to remember this in our schools, families, churches, and everywhere children are dealt with. Just as we need compassion for children, we need it for the rejected parts of ourselves in order to redeem them.

Jung stated that the shadow, the spirit of opposition that we meet whenever we turn inward, is 90 percent pure gold. A large part of what we think is evil within us is the pure gold of our naturalness waiting to be redeemed and only 10 percent is radical and irredeemable evil. The reasons for looking within are to find the gold and integrate it into our lives and to identify the parts of the evil that can't be saved, so we can be protected against them.

An example comes from my own puritanical background. Like so many others in our culture I was brought up to view the body and all sexuality as ultimately evil. My first lesson on sexuality came when I was five years old. My mother and I were walking downtown. We passed a little church with beautiful, stained glass windows on one side and a little brook running on the other. I asked my mother why Aunt Gertrude, who was unmarried, did not have any children. I immediately realized that I had stumbled into dangerous territory, truly the realm of the unmentionable. My mother could not be blamed for her attitudes. She was the daughter and granddaughter of Puritan ministers. All the lessons I received at home from the rest of the family reinforced this point of view. These attitudes on the subject went so deeply into me that I was thirty-three before I ever talked seriously about it to anyone, in this case, a Jungian analyst.

This rejection of my natural sexuality extended to the body itself and this became part of my shadow. I neglected the care of my body. Why should I exercise if the body is an ugly, awful thing? Now I have learned to appreciate that we are made in the image of God, and we are beautiful.

When they are repressed, the body and instincts react negatively causing all sorts of problems.

Radical evil finds a place of entry in me whenever I reject what God has created within me. There is certainly no better way to become neurotic than to try to become pure spirit. This denies the goodness of God's creation. The largest part of shadow is merely the natural I repress within me, which becomes, however, the entrance for the real evil that can wipe me out. I must be careful not to think my body or my instincts are evil. That is the Evil One's ploy to distract me from my destiny to become a whole person. When I deny a portion of God's creation within me, I create havoc and pain. This inner pain is the shadow calling for my attention like a rambunctious child. I need to keep an eye on my shadow, my darkness. In order to separate the aspects of my shadow that are inescapable parts of me from others that are due to the Evil One, I have to look at myself in the presence of Christ and make the distinction between the two. This is called discernment.

Many modern people believe that radical evil disappeared when we became wise enough to know that we will most likely not meet the Evil One in a red suit with a forked tail, horns, and a pitchfork. I hope that these people do not run headlong into the evil they deny. For myself I only wish that I knew the angelic with the same clarity with which I have experienced the demonic. I know only too well the reality of that which would drag me inwardly down into the pit, whispering into my ear all the time that I am valueless and that the world would be a fairer place if it were rid of my presence. I know the dark voice that tries to lure me into fragmentation rather than leading me on the high road toward holiness and wholeness. When asked if I believe in evil I reply in Jung's manner, "No, there are some things that are too important to be just the subject of belief. I *know* evil."

God seems to have made us half-beast and half-angel. What a sense of humor God must have. Our task is to unite these two aspects of ourselves in perfect harmony. This is quite an undertaking and it is no wonder that we sometimes repress one or another element of ourselves. Often our inner uncomfortableness is calling attention to the fact that we have not yet succeeded in accomplishing this merger and that we need to use discernment and reassess the situation. It also helps tremendously to have an accepting friend or guide or fellowship to help us in this process of discovering and integration. There is no more important task for the Christian church and clergy than this one.

The incarnation and atonement proclaim the Good News that God in Christ has defeated the powers of evil. Thus we need have no fear of the evil that we unmask. Jesus defeated evil on the cross once and for all, and we can share in that victory. How much less terrifying this makes the inner journey.

Possession, Evil, and Exorcism

There are some people in the church who find evil lurking behind every bush and every bed. They seem to have forgotten that the victory has been won. They view other people who do not behave just as they think they should as possessed of evil or by the Evil One. They make it their self-appointed task to deliver people from that bondage through exorcism or a deliverance ministry. This can be very dangerous, particularly for weaker people who fall under their domination.

In one book on deliverance an example is cited of a young man who should have had exorcism and because it was not given, murdered several people. However, this was obviously a case of psychosis. The person needed not exorcism, but the kind of loving counseling that could have given him control of the murderous impulses that all of us have within us. His psychic bottle was inadequately corked and he needed the development of a stronger ego or custodial care so he would not harm himself or another. There are genuine cases of possession, but they are very rare.

I have been open to the subject of possession for over thirty years and have been willing to see anyone who needed exorcism and to offer that sacramental action. But in all these years I have never seen a genuine classical example of exorcism. Brother Toby McCarroll is the founder of Starcross Monastery, near my home on the California coast. He was a psychologist before he found his religious vocation. His observation is the same as mine: most cases described as possession are little more than psychological disturbances. A psychological world view and some experience in clinical psychology could prevent a lot of damage done by ministers of deliverance, for these actions can have a profound, and not always good, effect upon people. Again the best ministry of deliverance is unconditional love and caring combined with psychological expertise.

Most people who talk about exorcism and deliverance also seem to believe that the Holy Spirit will only work through them and their actions. They also appear to attribute more strength and pervasiveness to the powers of evil than powers of God.

An example may help to clarify this matter. At the age of seventeen, a young man much in love and quite immature found that in spite of precautions his young woman friend was pregnant. The boy went along with her decision to have an abortion. Both of them were of Catholic upbringing and they went through it without talking to anyone. His bad conscience festered within him, and he rejected his sexuality unconsciously.

When he next entered into a committed intimate relationship with a woman, he was plagued by premature ejaculation.

Most practitioners of exorcism or deliverance would have caused further damage by speaking of the demon of sexuality and trying to exorcise it. Instead, as I talked with him about this matter he began to see that the right and wrong of it were different than he thought. Getting the young woman pregnant was indeed unfortunate and caused real harm. But it was the consequence of his immature pride and irresponsibility, not of sexuality as such. His misuse of sexuality had to be rejected, but this left room for its responsible use, and as he saw this, he was healed of his problem and the depression which had gone along with it.

As we develop the virtue of compassion and care, we must be aware that we do not fall into the opposite evil of being foolhardy and allowing others to take advantage of us. Some people prey on Christian convictions within a nominally Christian society. As canon of the cathedral in Phoenix, Arizona, one of my responsibilities was to administer the church's welfare monies. Phoenix was one of the great stopovers for drifters and swindlers, some of whom told me the most remarkable stories. One wise person suggested that I ask for a reference from each person so that I could confirm the story I was told. If the story turned out to be genuine, even though it usually involved a long-distance phone call, the person deserved some help; if it were not I found that they usually beat a hasty retreat. My work was immeasurably lightened as the word soon got around that the clergy at the cathedral were not gullible. To donate on the basis of a good story is naive, not compassionate.

Discernment means being circumspect with both the inner and outer world. An innocent-looking hitchhiker may be a hoodlum. People refuse to stop at the scene of an accident for fear of being set up or involved. Yet that there are exploiters of the innocent does not mean that we should never trust another. We need to use our own judgment and then ask the Lord for His guidance. One friend seldom prayed for healing for another until she stopped and asked in listening prayer if this was indeed her responsibility. We need to develop the same attitude towards both the inner and outer world.

One other feature of compassion that is often forgotten by those who have little psychological experience is that we should not impose our religious convictions on others before we are invited to. It has been said that the eleventh commandment is, "Do not remove your neighbors' boundary stone." This applies, I am sure, to inner boundary stones as well as outer ones. Inconsiderate pushing of opinions on others converts very few people and is a lack of trust in the truth and power of the Holy Spirit.

The Self

Jung maintains that we can observe the healing action of the self if we will open our eyes to it and give it more access to our lives. A German priest in one of my classes pointed out to me the significance of the term *Das Selbst,* which Jung used for this helping reality, this aspect of things that urges and helps us towards wholeness and integration. When I used the German term in class, his eyes brightened and he said, "Yes, I see, Jung is not talking about my own self, but is using the German neuter form of the word. This should be translated from the German as 'the itself.' " It is that which exists in itself apart from me. The word conveys something of the Biblical meaning of Yahweh's name, "I am that I am."

Sometimes this reality, which we might call the Holy Spirit or divine grace, works within us unconsciously, but our safest path is to search for the operation of this archetypal reality within us and to cooperate with it. Jung cannot explain the action of this reality, but he spent much of his life trying to describe it. Jung believed that we are naturally in contact with the self. Far from removing the possibility of transcendence, Jung suffuses our natural life with the glow of the divine. Jung had no ax to grind for Christianity or religion; he was convinced that it was his duty to describe reality as it presented itself to him, and the self was part of it. It is reassuring to find that from a purely scientific vantage point, Jung can describe the process of salvation that many of us have experienced. Nearly all of his later books deal with the self and how we come to allow it to become effective in our lives.

The ego has a very important function in this process. My psyche at times seems like a battlefield of opposing cosmic forces. I must choose which of these forces I will follow and then learn to follow with all the wisdom and will that I can muster. The Holy Spirit is seeking to draw me into the orbit of love and transformation, to bring me to unity and wholeness, to help me achieve my eternal destiny. But there is an opposing force that is trying to block me. I need to examine my life daily and see which way I am going and which way I wish to go and then renew my determination to follow the difficult path toward wholeness.

Jung found himself in a difficult position because of the idea of the self. According to the scientific community caught in meaningless determinism, Jung was spouting heresy and illusion and so he was largely rejected. He also alienated most of the theologians who maintained that only faith gives access to the spiritual realm. They resented what they considered his encroaching on their territory. Now, more than twenty years after his death people are just beginning to perceive the significance and importance of what Jung had to say.

Psychology or Spiritual Direction

Many theologians are afraid that psychologists will reduce religion and religious belief to "mere" psychology. And many psychologists have been burned by judgmental and rigid churches with no psychological insight and are afraid of religious influences. Are healings of the soul spiritual or psychological? This is an important question that must be answered. The answer is quite simple when we have a world view large enough to encompass the experience of the nonphysical world.

It is self-evident that everything that I experience is, in a sense, psychological. Take, for instance, this chair before me. All that I experience of this chair, whose reality I doubt in no way, is psychological. How I experience it—its color, texture, shape, esthetic value, size—is a function of my senses and of my capacity to synthesize all these discrete impressions into a pattern. We have learned that certain words stand for certain impressions but we are never sure that our impressions are the same as those of other people. Expert wine tasters have developed a language by which they can communicate their sense experiences. Likewise, when I am talking with people who have experienced rich religious lives, we can find words for common experiences that enable us to communicate and understand each other. As all experience comes through my psyche, it is literally psychological.

Most people will agree that the physical chair has a reality in itself; most people who have had significant religious experience will affirm the existence of the nonphysical reality that is called God. My experience of healing and being given meaning and tranformation is an experience of being touched and remade and rescued by something outside of me. Although healing comes through the psyche and uses it, Jung maintained that the simplest explanation or hypothesis is that we have encountered the self, or the divine. He affirmed that we can observe the action of divine grace naturally, but this does not make it natural. It operates in our natural world. If our eyes are open, we can see it. God is not as invisible as some people have believed, and certainly no more invisible than subatomic particles. We can experience the effects of the divine action and know the presence of God in a very real way.

Freud was a ground-breaking thinker and a very caring person, a man of immense literary talent and personal charm. But he provided no psychological avenue or mechanism for the action of the holy. With regard to religion, he came into a dead-end street. Nonetheless, probably more than any other person, he shook the world and prepared the way for getting out of the space-time box. He opened a road for others to travel further. We have already seen how little his model needed to be changed by Jung in order to provide an adequate base for understanding the full range of data which Jung studies. Like Jung, he felt himself to be more a midwife in the process of psychological development than the shaper of it, but he was unable to perceive the action of something beyond the soul involved in the process.

It is certainly clear that what Jung describes as the individuation process is very similar to what is described by the church as spiritual development and growth. But when I was in my own inner turmoil, I could find no one in the church to lead me on the way. Basically, the purposes of psychiatry and clinical psychology are quite different from those of spiritual direction. The person who comes to a marriage counselor, a pastoral counselor, or psychological expert is usually in pain; the pain can be caused by a chemical imbalance in the brain, childhood sexual traumas, inadequate personal relations, or being out of touch with the source of meaning and holiness. The clinical purpose is to get rid of the pain.

People who seek a spiritual director may indeed have some pain, but they are motivated by the goal of bringing the whole of their lives into congruence with God. If they need to change psychologically to achieve this goal, then this is part of the process. If they must look at their shadow and work at times of meditation, that is part of the process. To bring the totality of the psyche to God's transforming influence, one must know the entire psyche as deeply as possible. It is almost ludicrous to talk about spiritual direction that does not involve our sexual activities, our power motives, our treatment of our children, as well as ways of opening ourselves to the experience of God. Real transformation comes from touching the numinous and living out the implications of this encounter. The spiritual director who has little knowledge of the depth and range of human problems is indeed handicapped and may even do mischief; likewise, the psychological counselor who does not realize that a great deal of modern neurosis is caused by being cut off from the meaning that only a loving God can provide. Therapists who do know that a lack of vital religious experience may cause psychological problems are letting their clients down. And a recent survey by a friend and former student of mine, Timothy Kochems, shows that a large number of therapists are not comfortable dealing with the religious issues and avoid them.

Some people have come to me seeking spiritual guidance and ended by talking about their sexual anxieties. Some have come with apparently psychological problems and we mapped out a religious journey together. In my own counseling I do not use Jungian analysis as such. I use many of his methods, which put me in touch with similar disciplines used by spiritual directors throughout the ages. Jung's insights into the complex structure of the psyche and into the possibility of dealing with spiritual reality in a concrete counseling situation are invaluable. Religion and the church forgot these insights and methods when our culture climbed into the energy-mass-space-time box and pulled the lid down tight.

A counselor who is essentially interested in guiding and facilitating people along the religious path, the way of individuation, can often become discouraged. Often patients will stop seeking professional help just at the moment when they stop hurting and are ready to take up a real spiritual pilgrimage. John Sanford and I have discussed this at great length and we agree that our most central interest as counselors is in walking with people on the inner journey.

Before clergy take up the role of the spiritual director, they should receive training in pastoral counseling. I am associated with the program of spiritual guidance that has been inaugurated at the San Francisco Theological Seminary in San Anselmo, California. Dr. Roy Fairchild, director of the Resource Center for Spiritual Disciplines, is convinced that spiritual directors require a background in pastoral counseling. Going on the inner journey is a perilous path, as evidenced from John Bunyan's *Pilgrim's Progress* to Scupoli's *The Spiritual Combat*. We need a knowledge of the psyche before we go on that journey or take others upon it.[2]

Consequently, I usually put up some resistance whenever someone expresses a desire to go on the way of direct encounter with God. I want the person to think about it very carefully and to weigh the dangers, since it is nearly impossible to turn back with impunity once the inner journey has begun. Whenever someone in a psychological or spiritual crisis calls for an appintment, I always try to arrange one as quickly as possible or refer them to someone else if I have no time available. Often making that call was a true crying out for help. However, I am very cautious about taking people into the depth of spiritual direction.

In *Memories, Dreams, Reflections,* Jung tells of a doctor who came for help and who had some very negative dreams. Jung saw that the person had a very weak ego. So when the patient said he wanted to discontinue therapy, Jung quietly let him go. Similarly, we should never pressure anybody to go on the inner journey. That can be extremely harmful. The spiritual venture should be freely decided upon, as a result of a sense of inner ripeness and necessity. As a helper to the process, I must also realistically recognize that I cannot take anybody along the path any farther than I myself have gone.

Qualifications for the Inward Passage

The first essential prerequisite for the inner journey is a strong, well-disciplined ego. The ego is what enables me to get around in the world, hence in my dreams it may be symbolized by an automobile. The logic of the unconscious is clear. An automobile enables me to get around in the world just as my ego does. I am being warned of something wrong in my ego attitude if in a dream I lose my car in a parking lot, or smash it in an accident, run out of gas, or find the brakes do not work. The ego is indispensable to my enduring the tensions of the outer world without falling apart. It enables me to withstand poverty, disappointment, a hard childhood, a bad boss, or disagreeable neighbors and still keep smiling. It is my capacity to deal with reality and to survive sanely. Without a strong ego, it is dangerous for me to play around with the inner world, which can swallow me ten times faster than the outer one. Some people are taught that one should turn one's ego over to God. In a sense this is true, but we cannot give away what we do not have. We must have a well-developed ego in order to turn it over to God.

The best way of clinically determining the strength of the ego, of our ability to deal with reality, is the inkblot, or Rorschach, test. In this test we are presented with ten different standardized inkblots and asked to tell what response they evoke in us, of what they remind us. If we respond with any answer other than "inkblot" we reveal the nature and structure of our own psyche. What we perceive in these cards we have projected upon them. Bizarre responses are very often a sign of inability to see reality as others do. In my own clinical work I gradually learned to distinguish between those in distress and those living on the edge of psychosis. There is no substitute for clinical experience in learning to evaluate ego strength. People who defy all the standards and customs of society raise concern about the strength of their ego development.

People who have had a psychotic break or who find it difficult to stay rooted in physical reality should not undertake the inner journey unless they are under the close supervision of a psychiatric expert. Often people in this category need medication to control their symptoms. Sometimes they need custodial care which only psychiatrists can provide. As spiritual directors, we should not take such people on the spiritual journey except in conjunction with a psychiatrist who recommends our involvement.

Many clergy have a need to be needed. People with weak egos and borderline schizophrenics can fill that need endlessly. Since my time and energy are limited I need to be realistic about devoting my attention to those people whom I can benefit the most. Clergy and lay counselors need to be discriminating about those with whom they spend their time in counseling. I have also discovered that people who are giving nothing in return for the counseling, whether in a tithe or service to the church or in payment for service to the counselor, seldom value what they receive. Extended counseling involves a great deal of time on the part of the guide and unless the matter is faced squarely and the counselor recognizes responsibility, the situation can go sour. Paying for counseling or guidance can be therapeutic in itself.

There is a very special ministry to people who are psychotic or approaching psychosis. Several interesting attempts have been made to allow people the opportunity to enter into the depths of their delusions and fantasies and to pass through them to health. This kind of work requires very special training as well as custodial care. Only people with knowledge, understanding, patience, and a calling should undertake this kind of work.

I mentioned earlier a woman referred to me by a psychiatrist. I suggested to her to stop looking inward and handle her darkness sacramentally: to get a cross and wear it around her neck at all times, to take Communion frequently, and to tell the evil to be gone whenever it attacked her. I would see her once every two or three months and she could call me at the office if the darkness seemed particularly oppressive. She was greatly relieved; she never slipped into mental illness. She overcame all sorts of darkness, including an unfaithful husband, without going on the inner journey.

The reason for this woman's plight leads us to another criterion for readiness to undertake the inner journey. The desire to follow this way must be intrinsic to the person and not motivated by a desire to imitate other people. This woman had many friends on the inner journey and felt that she must go that way because they were doing it.

At the beginning of the first counseling session I have with any person I find it important to state quite clearly that one visit does not indicate that we will continue to go on counseling indefinitely. Both the counselor and the counselee need to determine whether the relationship is mutually desirable. Explicitly clarifying this situation avoids a premature dependence on the counselor and hurt feelings if the circumstances are such that the counseling should not be continued. Likewise, it gives the person seeking counsel freedom to terminate without explanation.

When my wife entered analysis for her most productive period of self-discovery, the analyst told her that they would plan four sessions together. At the end of that time either of them could terminate the counseling without explanation. When my wife passed the four-week trial period and knew she was to continue she asked why the analyst had suggested this arrangement. Her counselor told her, "You are functioning quite well in the outer world. Your problems come from outer circumstances. There are times when this should not be interfered with and sometimes it is best not to discuss the reasons for my decision." Then she added, "It is much easier to take people apart than it is to put them back together again. Sometimes it is better not to be taken apart." At the same time the counselor set the length of their appointments, times she could be called and times she couldn't, and what should be done in case of an emergency.

As in virtually all counseling situations, individual sessions of spiritual direction should last no more than an hour. If the psyche knows that it has one hour, it can usually say what is necessary in that time. This time should be scheduled at the convenience of both parties. As a counselor or director, I must not allow myself to be imposed upon unnecessarily at any hour of the day or night. Such imposition would not contribute to my self-esteem and would set a precedent of unhealthy dependence for the other person.

One of my responsibilities as a spiritual counselor is to establish a network of dependable colleagues to whom I can refer people whose problems are beyond my competence or areas of interest. I can usually be of help only to a person with whom I feel comfortable. Sometimes I will see a person when there is an urgent need until I can make an adequate referral and sometimes I find that I must continue with that person indefinitely if there is no one to whom I can refer him or her or if a transference has developed. At Notre Dame a young man was referred to me who was brilliant but had deep self-hatred. After we developed a relationship there was no way to terminate and we worked productively for several years together. The most important criterion for the spiritual director is to do nothing that does not express genuine concern and caring, to stay within the orbit of love.

Self-discipline is necessary to a successful inward journey. Often in the counseling situation we are unable to detect the lack of well-developed habits of discipline. One brilliant young man came to see me at Notre Dame with anxieties about many things and in deep depression. He graduated with high honors from Notre Dame and went on to get a postgraduate degree at another university. Then he took a job. As we discussed his days at work he told me that he spent ten minutes working and then would drift off into daydreams or get up for a cup of coffee. One of his basic problems was that he was so brilliant he did not have to work as hard as others to get high grades in college. I had been misled by his college success and it took me four years to find out this root of his problems. Without discipline, he was still operating out of the unconscious. He was still caught in the web of the mother complex.

We need discipline to separate ourselves from the unconscious and discover a standpoint from which to deal with the unconscious. Working in analysis with Hilde Kirsch I did a great deal of active-imagination exercises and then saw her only once a month for several hours. I would send in the work I had done. One month I did not get any done and when we met she asked me why I had not sent it in. I replied, "I didn't feel like it." To this she replied: "Ah, Morton, now you are going to let the unconscious be your mother and run your life!" I never missed doing my work again.

The Benedictines have known the value of discipline over the ages. The Benedictines at Pecos know it well. It is a wise community, founded upon discipline. People who cannot develop discipline have no business there. This protects both the community and the individuals. Those who cannot come to real discipline have no business on the inner journey. Spiritual discipline is founded upon a well-ordered and strong ego given to the service of God.

The responsibility of going with another on the journey toward God demands patience. One cannot push another or force the Spirit. Sometimes several years pass before individuals develop enough trust to share their deepest fears and angers with me. Until these are faced and brought before God, we are impeded upon the inner way. I have discovered that buried in the heart of everyone I have ever known well are sexual fears and authority problems of monumental stature.

Involvement in spiritual growth is no excuse for refusing to deal with the practical outer world. We need to have our feet firmly planted on the ground and be quite aware of where we are and where we are going, and at the same time have our psyches open to God and determined by our spiritual destiny. We need to be able to deal with bank accounts, post offices, loan agencies, and telephone companies if we are to deal successfully with this world and be ready to take on the next one. Sometimes we encounter misfortune, but often we create our own bad luck. To use the inner journey as an excuse for avoiding the unpleasantness of dealing with the nastiness and hardness of the world is immoral as well as dangerous.

I most enjoy working with people who have achieved worldly success and who wake up one day realizing that they have missed a significant element in life. These people often make the greatest advances in the religious life, people like Gregory of Nazianzus, Basil the Great, Augustine of Hippo, and Ignatius of Loyola.

The sign of real success in the outer world is not how much money I make, but rather how mature my interpersonal relationships are. My maturity can be measured by my ability to love and be loved. If I am not lovingly related to wife, children, and friends, it means that I have not developed a healthy and strong personality. One of the classic definitions of a weak ego is the person who is incapable of genuine, deep relatedness. This lack reaches its extreme in people with severe mental illness. We often have the sense when we try to relate to the psychotic or the borderline schizophrenic that we are relating to a vacuum. In technical language, they are said to show shallow affect.

Another Way

For those people who have no desire to or should not go on the inner journey, there is another way to arrive at the same destination: the way of the sacramental life and institutional church. These people can receive the Eucharist daily, make frequent and searching confessions, and try to bring the totality of their lives into line with divine love, of which the Eucharist is the supreme symbol. They can study the Bible and integrate its spirit into their lives. They can participate in church fellowship. One of the tragedies of the Reformation is that only the Catholic church continued to provide a rich sacramental life. Even though Reformers like John Calvin received Communion daily, their followers have slipped away from this practice and most Protestant churches simply do not offer the sacramental way to their people. Likewise, few Catholics know the treasures of the Bible.

Jung has commented that the Reformation has robbed most Protestants of the sacraments and symbols that can help the sensation-type person on the way to God. Whatever else is available in most Catholic churches, the daily Eucharist is there for those who are intent on remaking their lives in the image of God. Jung himself said that being deeply in the bosom of a church that provides sacramentally for all of our psychic needs can bring us into the Kingdom of Heaven as quickly as the inner journey. Protestant churches need to reconsider the place of the sacraments in their life and fellowship.

Aptitude for spiritual development differs from person to person. Intuitive-type people very often find themselves blocked unless they have the freedom to go the inner way and have direction on this way. Sensation types, in contrast, are usually fed by the images, symbols, and rituals of the church.

Few books have moved me more in my life than Jung's *Memories, Dreams, Reflections.* I had been in analysis and had discovered within me much of what I have discussed here. Like Jung, I am an intuitive. This book was a turning point in my life and confirmed the validity of my own journey. Yet many extraverted sensation types, and some other types as well, read the book and hardly understand it. They had not experienced anything similar to what he experienced. This is no defect in them. God made us different and provided different ways for us to go. Therefore, it is extremely helpful to know our own type so that we can choose the religious path that is most appropriate to our individual needs. The next chapter presents an in-depth analysis of Jung's theory of psychological types and their importance in spiritual development.

Does Jung's Point of View Make Sense?

Let us try to answer the critics of Jung who say, "Jung has some very interesting ideas. But do they provide a sensible and cogent view of the world? Is his 'system' philosophically sound?" This is not the place to answer this question in detail. I have dealt with it in the first three chapters of *Prophetic Ministry* and in *Encounter with God*. But a short answer to these crucial questions is necessary before we go further in applying his practical ideas.

I mentioned earlier that Jung was very much influenced by Immanual Kant, who made a detailed and meticulous analysis of human experience in his *Critique of Pure Reason*. Let us return to the Kantian example of the chair, to which I referred earlier. My sense experience and consciousness give the chair the form in which I experience it. According to modern physics, the chair in itself is mostly empty space where particular configurations of subatomic particles are whirling about in a manner beyond our ability to imagine or conceive. To the extent that my perceptions of the chair are incorrect, I am led farther away from how it is in itself. Scientific methods of observation help overcome the deceptive biases of appearances. Yet ultimately, knowledge is created by the interaction of an object and a subject. Experience occurs in a realm that is an interface between the two, and must be analyzed as such.

Jung accepted this basic Kantian principle. He took it one step further and advocated the analysis of the psychic realm. Jung believed that in addition to the physical object and the conscious subject, there was another objective realm (to which the psyche was even more closely related than it is to the physical realm). This he called the psychoid realm, which we have described as the spiritual one. In this area of experience careful analysis is all the more necessary; appearances cannot be taken for granted. By analogy to the physical world, a pencil in a glass of water looks bent or broken, due to the refraction of light by the water. We learn that the pencil is still straight by touching it. Likewise, our perceptions of the spiritual world need to be weighed, compared, and analyzed.

We need to examine very carefully psychic traumas for which we see no cause, to discover if there have been influences of realities of which we have not been aware. At the same time, we need to look with critical discernment at our experiences of prophecy, vision, dreams, or voices. If people have been deceived into thinking that the earth was flat or that the sun went around it, how much more easily can we be deceived when confronted with spiritual reality. It took science many years to come to the truth of the earth's spherical shape and its place in the heliocentric system. Likewise, it has taken religion a long time to evolve adequate methods of dealing with spiritual reality. A good religion gives a critical method of assessing spiritual reality. Religion is science of the psychic, or spiritual, domain. Its purpose is to help us deal creatively with spiritual reality without being deceived or overwhelmed. From a psychological point of view and from a religious point of view it is my conviction that no religion of humankind offers as much maturity, health, and salvation as a deeply understood and truly followed Christianity.

For very good reasons, I am doubtful of anyone who starts a new religion. No one is going to be able to begin from scratch and discover all that is necessary to religious knowledge. This wisdom is given only in the accumulation of experience of the spiritual world and by direct encounter with God. Jesus came in the fullness of time, when the religion of the Hebrews had developed to such a point that he could build on its foundations. He would not have presumed to initiate a new religion all by himself, but rather he made two major changes in the old one. God knew creation well enough to know that this would be difficult enough for human beings to accept.

NOTES

1. One of the best summary accounts of these phenomena was given at Princeton by Robert G. Jahn, dean of the engineering school. It was published as a special issue of the *Princeton Alumni Weekly Bulletin* on December 4, 1978. Entitled "Psychic Process, Energy Transfer and Things That Go Bump in the Night," it describes the different categories of psychic phenomena, telepathy (getting information from other minds without physical contact), clairvoyance (observing events across space), precognition (perceiving the future), and animal ESP. Related to these perceiving abilities are psychokinesis (the influence of the psychic domain upon the physical), out-of-the-body experiences, and evidence for survival of human beings after death.

2. I am at present working on a book on spiritual direction. I have come to a slightly different conclusion. For once-born people, to use William James' phrase, there is a kind of spiritual guidance that does not require great psychological expertise. This book should be published within six months.

Chapter 7

PSYCHOLOGICAL TYPES
AND THE RELIGIOUS WAY

A central injunction of our Christian faith is that we love our neighbors as ourselves and that we love one another as Jesus loved us by his life, his teaching, his death and resurrection. In order to love one another, we need to understand and to appreciate one another. In Jung's formulations about psychological types and in later research based on those formulations, we find great resources to help us sustain the loving faith by which we aspire to live.*

Each of us is born a unique human being with a distinct way of acquiring and organizing knowledge. When we use the ways of taking in information or of perception that are best suited to us, we also come to a more developed spiritual life. Our unique inner potential for spirituality depends on our living in accord with our own unique personality type.

There are a variety of testing instruments that attempt to show the individual's temperament and psychological type. The danger of relying on any one test though, is that people tend to take it too seriously. A psychological-profile analysis can be helpful only if individuals read the results thoughtfully and decide to what degree the test is valid for them. Such tests are tools to help people understand what their basic makeup is.

Another difficulty with any psychological-profile test is that many people answer it according to how they think they "should" be, or according to how they wish they were. Yet the purpose of the test is to promote awareness of individual preferences. Each person has such preferences

*This chapter is taken from the transcripts of lectures which my wife, Barbara, gave at the Benedictine Monastery in Pecos, New Mexico.

instinctively, but consciousness of this most basic level is often over-shadowed by conditioning and the pressure to conform. Many people trained in religious orders by the old methods of education fail to record their instinctive preferences on the test. They were trained to perform according to the order's expectations. The only way to assure the most authentic answers is to respond to the questions as if nobody else would ever know how we responded.

One should never base an important life decision on the results of any one test. No psychological or sociological device has such validity. One needs to consider much more evidence. For example, in many schools children are categorized on the basis of a single IQ test. Yet the child could go into the test with a headache or just after a fight with a parent and not care at all about the test. About forty years ago, my very intelli-gent brother scored very low on an IQ test. Our mother had died and we had moved to a new city where he knew no one, and he was very upset. He made no effort to score highly. We should be cautious in reading the results of any test.

One test, the Myers-Briggs Type Indicator, is based on Jung's theory of types and aims to reveal whether a person has more highly developed thinking, intuitive, feeling, or sensation functions for relating to the world. It also discriminates extraverted from introverted preferences. Everybody uses all of those psychological functions some of the time, but we develop some more than others. Each one of us can benefit from recognizing what our psychological preferences are. At periods of our lives we may direct our attention to cultivating a neglected function. But people should de-velop their preferred function first so they can become what they were created to be. Interestingly, in order to use one function, we need to be able to learn to turn off the opposite one. For example, thinking (in the sense of logical thinking) and feeling (value-system thinking) block each other. Sometimes indecision indicates that a person has no clear prefer-ence of one function over another. In other words, the person really can-not decide whether to opt for logic (thinking) or for what seems right to them (value or feeling) to come to a decision.

As small children we use sensation, intuition, feeling, and thinking in a more or less equal distribution. As we grow, we learn to use one of these functions in a more refined and productive manner. That is the meaning of our growth: we specialize. We were actually born to be spe-cialists in one function and to cultivate a second to support the first. That second one is called an auxiliary function. When the auxiliary is devel-oped, we talk about being balanced. In referring to psychological func-tions, balanced does not mean using all the functions equally. In fact, John Sanford writes in his book *The Kingdom Within* that Jesus Christ was the only person who ever balanced all four functions. Most of us, however, eventually learn which function we prefer to develop.

Introversion and Extraversion

In discussing psychological types, the terms introversion and extraversion must be understood. Introversion means that the person prefers to deal with the inner world of ideas and concepts and finds his or her renewal of energy coming during a period of inward turning and aloneness. Extraversion means that one prefers to deal with the outer world of people and things and is energized by interaction with others. Of course, we all alternate between inner and outer attention. For example, my husband and I spent thirty-two weeks on the road giving conferences four years ago. This involved us in mostly extraverted behavior. Although we are both basically introverted people, we could do this because we knew ourselves well enough to protect ourselves and to schedule times to be alone. An extravert actually gets an infusion of energy from other people. An introvert's power comes from settling in and quieting down. Introverts tend to like quiet for concentration. They often have a poor memory for names and faces. They usually are careful with details. They are interested in the idea behind their jobs. They often dislike telephone interruptions. My husband and I used to stand and argue about who was going to answer the phone when it rang; we finally solved that problem by removing the phone from the house. Introverts like to think a lot before acting, and sometimes they think and think and then do not act. They work contentedly alone and sometimes have problems communicating. They often become infused with energy from being quietly alone. They can be alone some of the time without being lonely.

The interest of extraverts flows mainly to the outer world of actions, objects, and persons. They usually like variety and action. They dislike complicated procedures. They are often good at greeting people. They tend to be impatient with slow jobs. They do not mind the interruption of answering the telephone. They act quickly, sometimes without thinking. They like to have people around. Usually they communicate freely. Their energy seems to flow to them from people.

In the United States, we have more extraverts. In Switzerland it is the reverse. England and Japan are also supposed to be more introverted. I know of no studies that indicate whether these trends are inherited. There are observable national patterns, however.

An extravert can go to a party, have a good time until two o'clock in the morning, and leave feeling so invigorated that the principal thought in mind is, "Where can I find another party?" The introvert can go to the same party, have a good time, but leave an hour and a half later feeling totally exhausted. The introvert then needs to go home and quiet down in order to revive and have the energy to go on.

The differences between introversion and extraversion can be very important within families, friendships, and wherever social interaction and communication are involved. People usually judge one another on the basis of their own natures. Introverts know that they are at their best when dealing with their inner world of concepts and ideas. When they go out to meet others, they know that they are often on the defensive and their second-best qualities are operative. After the introvert gets to know and trust another person very well, sometimes after months, the inner side, which is more highly developed, is revealed. The other person can be amazed that such a depth was there. In contrast, the extravert comes across immediately with the more developed function. Later on in the relationship, the extravert may show the inner side, but it is not as highly developed.

How do these differences of type influence our evaluations of one another? The extraverts assume that first impressions of the introverts give the full picture. Consequently, when the introverts finally show their more highly developed inner side, the extraverts feel as if they had been deceived at first. He or she may ask, "Why weren't you more authentic? Why didn't you let me know what you were truly like? Why did you put up a false front?" Yet the introverts were being authentic from the very beginning, but functioning just as they were created by God to be. In turn, the introverts may be fascinated by first impressions of the extraverts and think, "I can't wait to get to know him or her better." But nothing better comes later. The introvert can be disappointed and mistakenly judge the extravert as shallow. In truth, both the introvert and extravert can be displaying the same depth, but directing it to opposite areas of life. We need to understand this about one another.

In our nation, the introverts comprise about 30 percent of the general population and the extraverts about 70 percent. In many religious groups, we find the introverts in the majority. A counselor or spiritual director ministers very differently depending on whether he or she is an introvert or extravert. Therefore the counselor or director needs self-understanding and a reliable assessment of another person's type in order to avoid imposing standards that do not fit. In families one sees how important a sense of psychological type can be. For instance, sometimes an introverted child is born to two extraverted parents and never receives the peace and quiet needed for his or her own healthy growth. The child is inundated with stimuli without being given the time or space for assimilation, and then is misjudged as stupid. An introverted individual's self-esteem can be damaged by constant pressures from a majority of extraverts to conform to behavior patterns that just do not suit that individual.

The Perceptive Functions: Sensation and Intuition

Sensation and intuition are two different ways we take in information about the world. They are called perceptive functions. A person with a predominating sensation function wants to perceive the world directly through the senses. Often the sensation type will be able to tell you exactly what color clothing another was wearing at a party months ago. This is usually not the case with intuitives. The sensation type lives in the present. "Yesterday is over; tomorrow may never come; right now is important." This expresses the attitude of the sensing person, who is usually very present when talking with another. For example, in the medical profession research has shown that the sensation type make good anesthesiologists, paying precise attention to all the dials and equipment and not missing any details necessary while they are monitoring the patient.

The sensation types get things done in the world. For them the only appropriate response to stimuli is action. If they hear about starving people in a ghetto somewhere, they want to go and feed them. They do not ask questions; they get busy. They need to find some enjoyment in their daily lives if they are to be satisfied and contented. For one, it might be reading, for another, dancing. Especially if the person is working strenuously, some small period each day should be scheduled for the preferred enjoyment.

Sensing types dislike new problems. They want a standard way of doing things. They are good at jobs requiring exacting observation, routine, and details. They like to learn a skill and then be able to use it. Often they prefer to continue developing that skill rather than to change to something else.

As little children, sensation types take fairy tales and mythology literally. They should not be told such tales unless the metaphorical sense is explained to them carefully in terms they can understand. They can be frightened without such an explanation. As they go on in school, they do not find fantasy novels or mythology to their liking. They prefer factual, linear thinking. They like jobs where they can do detailed work like checking records, reading proofs, or scoring tests. They are impatient when the details get too complicated. They rarely get inspired; inspiration does not usually motivate them. They give good reports of exactly what happened without adding in much interpretation. They want the solution to any problem to be workable. Their shadow or negative side is that they occupy themselves with suspecting all sorts of negative possibilities.

About 30 percent of the population are at least partially intuitive. That means intuition is either their main or auxiliary function. They live in the future. Their need is for inspiration and intellectual stimulation. They think of new possibilities.

The intuitive type takes in information indirectly, through the unconscious. The intuitive comes up automatically with possibilities and inferences connected with the information. An intuitive can hear the same facts stated as the sensing person. Whereas the latter will remember the facts but not necessarily know what to do with them, the former may not remember them but will often propose at least ten suggestions about what to do tomorrow on this basis of these facts! In reading these very words, the sensation type would try to stay with them and learn about typology. The intuitive is already wondering about what to do with it in the future.

Intuitives like solving new problems and dislike doing the same thing over and over again. They enjoy learning a new skill much more than using it and they are apt to make mountains out of molehills. They work in bursts of energy, powered by enthusiasm, with slack periods in between. As children, they take fairy tales metaphorically. They put two and two together quickly. They apply ingenuity to problems, dislike routine details, are good at problem-solving types of jobs, and are patient with complicated situations. They can look far ahead. They usually follow their inspirations, whether good or bad, and of this they must be careful. They often get their facts a bit wrong. They spark solutions to problems that seem impossible but they dislike taking time for details and precision. They put their faith in what is possible rather than in what is actually there. They want a door left open in any proposition for growth and improvement. They often can explain what another intuitive is talking about, as intuitives often start in the middle of things, and we don't know what the antecedent is. Another intuitive can sometimes make that jump where a sensation type would be at a loss.

A woman who attended one of my sessions reported that she and three colleagues were in danger of losing their jobs. After the lecture on psychological types, she realized why. She and her three colleagues were intuitives. Her boss was a sensing type. At staff meetings the four intuitives would communicate as much between words as in what they made explicit. The boss thought there was some collusion among them, as he never heard the facts to which they were alluding. For example, one would say, "I know who should do the job." The others exclaimed, "You're right." As they understood one another, they had no need to mention the person by name.

The shadow or negative side of intuition is often a crude seeking of pleasure. Intuitives also are apt to dawdle and procrastinate when their inspirations are at a low ebb. Note that the shadow side of the intuitive comes out of the unconscious sensation aspect. Likewise the shadow side of the sensing type comes out of the unconscious intuitive function. As those unconscious functions are more developed later in life, less shadow remains to cause problems.

In religious practice, it is essential to be aware of the sensation-intuition polarity. The sensation type cannot sit for hours of meditation or contemplation, but often feels that every speck of matter is infused with the spiritual. Although not all experiences are sent by God the sensation type needs to feel that God can be present with them in all experiences if called upon. We need only to pause and stand still and realize the divine presence. This is easier for the sensation type to understand than for intuitives. The prayer life of the sensing person often begins in finding the spiritual in a contactable way through the outer world. Therefore, the Eucharist or other rituals can be very beneficial. Preparing a dinner and serving others can be prayerful work for the sensation-type person. This should not be scorned by those of a different temperament.

A nurse or teacher can work prayerfully, beginning each day or session with a prayer, such as "Lord, I have the body of knowledge but do not know how to best use it. Please guide me." This may sound shallow to an intuitive, who relates to the divine in other ways. But the introverted sensing type needs to start prayer with something tangible, such as rosary beads, a verse in the Bible, a picture, even the smell of incense or some music. A nun from Africa once reported to me that she always had to start her prayers in such a way. Then she related it to whatever was going on in her life at that time. In the contemplative way, one starts with an outer experience, stays with it, reflects on it, and, hopefully, turns to its implications for one's life.

The extraverted sensing type of person will almost always be more interested in something like church finance rather than in doctrine. Whatever service they go to, they will be looking to see if the altar linens are properly ironed and folded in the right way or if the vestments are pressed. Such details are important to them. Thereby, they contact something meaningful. They are more interested in corporate worship than individual prayer. They can learn to put their individual prayers within the context of their corporate worship.

The introverted sensing type actually finds meaning in the externals. Even an inferior piece of art should be tolerated in churches if it is a means whereby some people contact a reality that would otherwise be inaccessible to them. They are often helped in their prayer life by copying from books of prayer the ones that are meaningful to them and then using these as the basis of their devotional life. Parts of Ignatian prayer are very good for the sensation type. For example, one puts oneself into a biblical story and imagines, for example, that one is Mary riding on the donkey, pregnant and uncomfortable. One then tries to connect that story with one's present life.

Having said all this about the types, we need to remind ourselves that no individual is purely one type. Each of us also has the auxiliary side developed. The only way for me to distinguish the functions intellectually is to talk about them separately, but when they combine together in real life the whole is greater than the sum of its parts.

The religious life of the introverted intuitive can be cultivated in various ways. Such a person can turn to a prayer manual and meet with success. The reason is that prayer manuals are usually written by introverted intuitives. They constitute, according to David Kiersey and Marilyn Bates in their book *Please Understand Me*, only 4 percent of the entire population of the United States, yet their prayer manuals are assumed to be usable by everyone. This can cause serious problems. Sometimes after I lecture someone comes up to me to say, "I have been in a religious community for twenty years, and I always thought something was wrong with me because I couldn't do what they were talking about as the inner journey. It never had any real meaning to me. Now I know I'm alright. My journey has to be to find the inner through the outer."

For intuitives, the words growth and change have a very warm positive meaning. Most sensation types do not consider change important or pleasant. They prefer to learn something well, to become specialists who keep taking in the latest information in the field and developing it. By contrast intuitive-feeling types, according to Kiersey and Bates, set as a life goal the finding of a life goal. At times they get a goal for their lives and then keep putting off finalizing it until it is replaced by another. Sensation types do not understand this. They want to develop their established career, not to undergo continuous change.

In a marriage, confusion and conflict can arise if one partner has a sensation orientation, the other an intuitive one. The intuitive can feel held back by the partner, complaining that the other does not want to move, change, or be creative. It is important in counseling not to encourage intuitives to open up and explore growth without cautioning about the repercussions and negative possibilities this could have on their outer life and relationship. It is good if the intuitive can be accompanied by the sensation-type partner to any growth experience they decide to participate in so the sensation-type partner is able to get an accurate report about what actually happened. Intuitives are not usually good at reporting what actually went on without interpreting it and giving their conclusions about it. If the partners are very different perhaps they can learn to leave each other alone without trying to change each other, and will be able to see each other as peers with differences. This is better than fighting to make each other into what they can never become.

To summarize up to this point, sensation and intuition are two distinct ways of learning about the world. We call them perceptive functions.

The Judgmental Functions: Feeling and Thinking

The next question is, How do we organize what we take in or perceive either by sensing or intuition? This depends upon our judgmental functions. The term judgmental is not used in a moralistic sense. It refers to that faculty which gives a sense of proportion, fittingness, order. With this faculty we reach our decisions, either by using our values, which is called feeling, or by using our logic, which is called thinking. These two terms are not used in their ordinary sense. Feeling is the function of using value systems to think through to conclusion. In more ordinary English, this would not be called feeling. It is clearly a rational function, and Jung calls it that. In this Jungian sense, feeling does not refer to emotions. People who score high on the feeling scale in the Myers-Briggs Type Indicator may indeed be more in touch with their emotions, but the test does not directly look into that question. Rather, it examines whether a person uses a value system to come to conclusions. A thinking person uses cause-and-effect logic to reach decisions, whereas the value system takes one's own self and others into account. The feeling types, by my definition, think in terms of what is worthwhile to others and themselves. Both sorts of judgmental functions are valid; both are needed in any organization; both need to be present to some degree in our lives. However, the two judgmental functions cannot be used at the same time. Sometimes a client comes for counseling who is characterized by chronic indecision. Often such a person needs to be advised to develop either utilitarian cause-and-effect logic, or human considerations. In organizations, the thinking types tend to go to the top.

About 50 percent of the population are feeling types. However, there are more females than males among them: 60 percent of this group is female and 40 percent is male. This may be culturally determined. In a work situation, if there are any interpersonal feuds going on, the feeling types lose a great deal of their efficiency. By contrast, thinking types lose little of theirs and are hardly aware of the feuds. If there is a disagreeable, conflict-ridden atmosphere thinking types can carry on without getting upset. But feeling types like harmony and let their decisions be influenced by their own and other people's likes and wishes. They need occasional praise, and sympathy. It helps them if someone acknowledges the difficulties and pains they suffer. They dislike telling people unpleasant things. They can persuade, conciliate, forecast how others feel. They arouse enthusiasm. They can teach, sell, or advertise. They can help the thinker's self-appreciation. Thinkers have real trouble feeling themselves worthy and need to be told often how well they are doing. Feeling types relate well to most people. They tend to be sympathetic. They need a job that demands a tactful handling of people. They evaluate from a personal angle, that is, in terms of how something affects human beings. They want the solution to any problem to be agreeable. Their shadow or negative side is a crudely domineering type of thinking, accepting a whole system and trying to force it on everybody else. This probably comes out of the unconscious and undeveloped thinking function.

The thinking types are 50 percent of the general population: 60 percent are male and 40 percent female. Historians are often of this type. Their time perception is logically in past, present, and future. It is a personal affront for the thinking type when their own original ideas are not accepted. If one cannot accept a thinking type's ideas, it is advisable to preface the criticism with a few complimentary remarks on other areas one genuinely appreciates. For the thinking type, not having thoughts accepted is comparable to being ridiculed. Thinkers are the least flexible of all types in their ideas. They are relatively unemotional and appear uncaring about other people's feelings. They prefer organization and do not like a lot of talking. If one is living with a thinking type, there is much more harmony if one does not chat and converse casually.

Thinkers often hurt people's feelings, usually without knowing it. They do not mean to do it. They benefit if they can work closely with feeling types so that others' emotions or values can be interpreted for them. They enjoy putting things in logical order, and they like analysis. They can get along without harmony. They often state their position bluntly and they tend to decide impersonally, ignoring people's wishes. They are often critical. As children, they like things to follow logically from causes. They have a great need to understand whatever is said to them. Their great wish is to be treated fairly. Therefore they need to be listened to so that their definition of fair can be understood.

To show thinking types love, one treats them fairly within their personal definition of what is fair. They often need jobs that require an impersonal approach. They can reprimand and fire people when necessary. This is important in organizations. For feeling types, it is traumatic to have to fire someone. A thinking type, however, if the decision is fair, can fire someone and lose no sleep over it. Thinking types relate best to other thinkers. They can talk together without worrying about one another's feelings. They weigh the law and evidence in any situation and can hold firmly to a policy against opposition. They want the solution to any problem to be systematic. Their shadow is explosively unruly feelings out of all proportion to what triggers them. This comes from their unconscious feeling function, which tends to keep them out of contact with their inner responses and thus their emotions can build up as in a pressure cooker.

Orientation to the Outer World: Perceptive or Judgmental

To distinguish perceptive from judgmental types reveals differences in lifestyle. The perceptive types are those who use their sensation or intuition in the outer world, and this function is what others first encounter in them. People who are perceptive in their outer lifestyle are judgmental in the inner, and vice versa. We all have both areas in ourselves. The perceptive types tend to be good at adapting to changing situations. They do not mind leaving things open to alternatives. But they often have trouble making decisions. If two perceptive types live together, a typical conversation may go like this: "Where do you want to eat out tonight?" "Oh, I don't know. What about you?" "I don't know." Perceptives often start too many projects and have trouble finishing them, especially if they are also intuitives. Perceptives may postpone unpleasant tasks. They want to know all about a new job or new place before going to it. They tend to be curious and to welcome new light on a situation or person. *They are process oriented.* The goal is not as important as the process of getting there. Every day should have some meaningful activities.

The judging types relate to the outer world with either feeling or thinking. They are best when they can plan their work and follow the plan. They like to get things settled and wrapped up. They ere apt to cut off any new input or information because they do not want their system upset or changed. They may reach decisions too quickly. They dislike interrupting one project for a more urgent one. They may not notice new things that need to be done. They want only the essentials. They tend to be satisfied once they have reached a decision. *They are goal oriented.* In fact, they have a goal for the day, the week, their job, and even for recreation. They often come to conclusions without considering new information or enough data.

Here is a personal anecdote to illustrate the difference between judging and perceptive types. When my husband and I were first married (during World War II), we were both working twice as much as at any other time in our lives. I was a social worker for the Red Cross and also taught school. Morton had a parish and did other things on the side. We could look ahead to one day in every three or four weeks as our day off. Often our dinner conversation was entirely on the subject of what we would do with that precious day. Being perceptive, I looked forward to sleeping late, then getting up and seeing what I felt like doing. Morton dreamed of awakening bright and early, cleaning up the dirty house, shopping for the coming week, doing the laundry, going on a picnic for one hour and forty-five minutes, and coming home to work on our souls for an hour or two. Morton planned our day of leisure minute by minute. Although this was before the women's liberation movement, I felt that there was something that did not suit me. We compromised. Once in eight weeks we did it my way, and once in eight weeks his way. That is how a judgmental and perceptive type can live together.

Isabel Myers, the creator of the Myers-Briggs Type Indicator, died in 1981. She devoted her entire career to developing Jung's typology. Shortly before her death, she corrected the page proofs of her book *Gifts Differing*, which is the most readable and definitive volume on the subject of typology. The author observed that judgmentally oriented people are apt to look at perceptive people as aimless drifters. The perceptives are likely to look at the judgmental types as only half alive. For perceptives, the information is never all in. They do not want to finalize their views because they know that tomorrow new information could change the situation. Judgmental people want to make up their minds and stick to their decisions. They do not like extra information and can be annoyed by it. A case in point is that of a clinical psychologist who some years ago attended one of my lectures, bought a book, and went on to base her clinical practice on it. Later, she attended another recent lecture I gave and was very upset when I discussed the shortcomings of the book. She was irritated that now she would have to change the basis of her practice.

Insights into the Various Types

Gifts Differing points out the dangers of the different types. The sensation type runs the risk of becoming frivolous and can get caught in seeking enjoyment. The intuitive can become fickle, running from one romantic affair to another. They are often changeable and often lacking in persistence. These conditions can be controlled by the development of the feeling or thinking functions to a higher degree.

In a religious context, feeling types would like to hear sermons or homilies addressed to the heart as part of their corporate worship. They like periods of silence, to be able to ingest what is said. If worship services do indeed include such periods of silence, it is important for the nonfeeling types to be instructed about what to do with the silence. This is not always self-evident. Thinking types always need to understand the reasons for things. They do not want to accept a situation just as an experience as do the feeling types.

I am a feeling type and once team-taught in a junior college class with a woman who was a thinking type. We balanced each other. Once we went to a Holy Thursday service together. I was enchanted by the candle light, the stripping of the altar and other ceremonial proceedings. But throughout the service, the other woman was writing. I was irritated by the noise that this made as it distracted from an immersion in the mystery of the service. Finally, at the end, I asked my friend, "What were you writing about?" She answered, "I had the most wonderful idea. All of our students went to a Holy Thursday service, too. In class we can explain to them exactly what all the symbolism meant from beginning to end." I said, "You are going to kill it. I don't want to understand everything. I just want to experience something like this that is meaningful to me." In class we compromised and explained some of the symbolism but left it for the students to work the rest out for themselves if they wished or just to experience what they had experienced. I have a feeling orientation; my colleague relied on her thinking. This story shows how difficult communication can sometimes be between the two types. Thinking types want to understand what they have experienced and the feeling types just want to experience the experience.

Thinking types often appear cold and distant to the feeling types. Yet they may be as sensitive underneath and easily hurt. They are just not as aware of other people's feelings. How other people feel is not part of the formula upon which their system is based. The thinkers question whether something is true. The feelers want to know whether it is right and agreeable.

The following story illustrates some characteristics of the value dimension of the feeling function. Once upon a time, there was a river. It was full of alligators, and very wide. On one side, there lived a young girl named Mary. On the other side, there lived a young man named John. A bridge crossed the river. Mary and John played together as children. As youths they teased each other. As teenagers they held hands together on the bridge. One day they looked into each other's eyes and found they were in love. They planned a marriage. But suddenly there was a big storm that washed the bridge away. They cried and waved to each other from the opposite banks of the river.

Eventually, a young man named Steve came down the river in a boat. He went to Mary and asked why she was crying. She looked at his boat and asked if he could take her across the river to John. He said he would take her across only if she met his needs. She asked, "What are your needs?" He said, "To have sexual intercourse with you." Mary said, "Well, I don't know about that." He said, "I don't want to push you, so I will come back tonight for my answer. Unless you let me have sex with you, I will not take you across the river." Mary was in a turmoil.

She remembered an old woman who lived in the forest and was reputedly wise. Her name was Martha. Mary went to Martha's hut to see if Martha could help her decide what to do. Martha invited her in, expressed concern for her, and offered her tea. "What's your problem?" Martha asked. Mary said, "A young man propositioned me, and I don't know what to do. Tell me what to do." Martha responded, "I can't tell you what to do. You have to decide for yourself."

Mary wandered home just as upset as ever. That night she went to the river undecided and finally invited Steve in for the night. The next morning he took her across the river.

John was overjoyed. They hugged and kissed. He said, "We have to go get married." She said, "You don't know what I had to go through to get here." She told him about Steve. John was shocked. He said, "You cheap woman. How could you sell yourself so cheaply?" She answered, "John, I did it for you." But he exclaimed, "I never want to see you again." She cried, "But John, I am on this side of the river. Where can I go?" He said, "I don't care. I just never want to see you again." She was shocked and went into the forest crying.

Out of nowhere another young man named David came along. David asked her what had upset her. She told him the whole story and then said, "I wish you would go and kill John." David said, "You stay here. I will take care of him." He beat John up and came back to marry Mary. They lived happily ever after.[1]

Among Christians who listen to this story, there is no consensus in evaluating the correctness of each character's actions. This suggests that there is no one Christian value system. Each person has a unique value system with different priorities. Some people will rank Mary highest because they value innocence. Others will put her in the last slot because they see her as stupid. Those who liked Steve saw value in his stating openly and honestly what he wanted. Others disliked him for taking advantage of Mary's predicament. Martha was judged negatively by those who thought she had a duty to point out the consequences of the different options and to help Mary decide. Others thought Martha was right to keep out of the problem. People opposed to violence disliked David. Those who thought John got what he deserved put David in first place.

The kinds of issues involved here go beyond the logical step-by-step procedures of instrumental thinking: This story shows the complexity of the feeling function. Feeling types think with their value system, and not with logic.

Another approach to the four functions is through time studies. The sensation type lives in the now. The intuitive lives in the future and consciously has to plug in sensation to be present to another person in conversation. One Methodist minister spoke of his future orientation and how it sometimes angered his wife. All year long he works at planning his family reunion. Yet when it finally arrives, he is already thinking about the next year's celebration and does not even want to be present for the festivities. This is an extreme example of the intuitive's time orientation. As the wife was another type, it was incomprehensible to her.

The feeling type relates to time in a circular way. Thinking types find this the hardest time sense to grasp. The feeling type starts in the past with a meaningful experience, and wants to duplicate it in the present. For example, a feeling person who had a pleasant home life as a child tries to make the present home life pleasant in the same way. If as a child one was given cookies and milk after coming home from school, one tries to make this same treat available to one's own children.

If we think about Christmas, the significance of the feeling type's relation to time and the past becomes all the more poignant. There is a story about a feeling type who joined a religious order and stayed away from the parental home for twenty years and then decided to go back one Christmas. All the way there, an expectation grew of Christmas as it used to be. There was a green tree with multicolored lights. A festive dinner of roast goose was served on Christmas Eve. Presents were opened in the evening. Then the family went out to midnight mass together. Imagine how the feeling type coped with the following homecoming: There was a white plastic Christmas tree with blue lights. Leftovers were served for dinner. No presents were opened. That could be taken care of the next day. The parents went to bed early. The now grown-up child asked, "What about midnight mass?" The parents said, "We don't see so well now and cannot go out driving at night. We can go to church in the morning." Despite the intellectual level of acceptance on the part of the feeling type, there was a deep underlying nostalgia for the past, and a sense of loss. Each missing element multiplied the sense of poignant melancholy.

Counselors often find the feeling types tend to repeat negative experiences from the past. One woman was married to an alcoholic for years and finally divorced him for the children's sake. She stayed alone for years and then met another man whom she found sensitive and to her liking. She decided to marry him and found out that he, too, was an alcoholic.

This is common. We tend to repeat negative experiences unless we become aware of our unconscious patterns.

The thinking type is as logical about time as about other things, able to relate to past, present, and future. The past gives valuable information that helps one decide in the present and project into the future.

When one is presenting a plan that requires broad approval to a group of people, there are some pointers to keep in mind for appealing to the four types. For the sensation type, a project must be workable. One needs to indicate where the money is coming from, who is going to do the work, how long it will take. For the intuitive, one has to leave a door open for inspiration, growth, and improvement. For the thinking type, the presentation must be systematic. For the feeling type, it must be humane.

When people develop their functions regularly, the third function may operate adequately by the middle of life. It is always in service of the dominant function. In periods of crisis or change, a person may prefer one of the less developed functions. For example, an intuitive who never did much handiwork may, in a period when life seems dull, take up an enthusiastic interest in painting, which is a sensation-oriented activity. Anything that is unconscious in a person tends to be undeveloped. When that aspect comes out spontaneously, it is likely to be rather primitive. For an intuitive type, sensation is in the unconscious. When it emerges, it does so primitively as an aspect of the shadow. This is characterized often by a low order of pleasure seeking, by procrastinating, and by showing a lack of inspiration when energy seems to be lacking. The sensation type has intuition in the unconscious: When that emerges it is in the form of negative intuitions and hunches that are almost always wrong. Nothing worries me more than to hear a lecturer say to a group of people, "Now you have to learn to trust your hunches and intuitions." This could cause a sensation type to jump off a bridge some night. Such a type has to learn that his or her intuitions may not be trustworthy.

The feeling type has the greatest trouble with cause-and-effect thinking. When the shadow emerges, that type can take an idea and start telling it to everyone who comes along, whether they want to hear it or not. The feeling type can get stuck on an idea because he or she lacks a developed critical-thinking side.

Thinking types do not develop sensitivity to the feelings of others, nor are they in touch with their own. If they are in a sensitivity training group, it is wrong to expect them to be able to give a "gut" reaction to how they are feeling at the moment. They may not know until a few days later how they feel at any given time. The thinking type's shadow can emerge with explosive, unruly feelings, out of proportion to an event.

Resentment builds up in this type, which makes its shadow potentially dangerous.

There are spiritual fruits in each developed function. For the sensation type of person, it is simplicity of life and lifestyle. For the intuitive, it is wisdom. Intuitives know, but do not know how they know. For the feeling type, the spiritual fruit is the ability to experience joy. Many other types are not able to have this experience. (But one should be careful with joy. It can be dangerous to impose it on someone who is depressed. If a person is in a pathological depression, it makes matters worse to be around joyful people. The depressed need someone to hold hands with and sympathetically cry with them.) For the thinking type, justice is the fruit. In the Roman Catholic church, the thinking types are usually at the top of the hierarchy. They develop a plan for justice and expect those in the field to implement the plan.

Decision making can be facilitated if one knows one's type, and tries to bring all functions to bear on the decision. Sensing comes first, although it is particularly difficult for the intuitives to use. It means finding out every fact relevant to the decision, positive and negative. These should be written down. Others should be consulted for their assessment of the facts. The next quality to use is intuition. One asks what the implications are of each one of the facts. The third function to be called on is thinking. This involves looking into the consequences of the decision. The feeling type tends to avoid facing negative and unpleasant consequences. The feeling type should therefore go to a thinking type to hear the potential negative consequences, trying not to get too upset about it. At the last stage of decision making, the feeling function comes in. How much is this choice worth to myself, to humankind, to the world, to the church, to God? That is the question of feeling. For the ultimate decision, after looking into the contributions of each of the four functions, we return to the dominant one, which is enriched by the others.

Isabel Myers asserts that when dealing with people, especially with children, one needs to relate on the basis of one's own perceptive function (sensation or intuition). Nothing causes more trouble to children, she claims, than to be handled with the judgmental thinking or feeling function. It is tragic when a child is brought up under pressures to be something other than what his or her own nature needs; this is different from expecting the child to be who he or she is but asking them to increase their present level of actualization. The judgmental person must be careful not to try to program a child into feeling required to do the impossible: always be on time, always be clean, always be polite. Sometimes people in their sixties come up after one of the lectures on psychological types and express the relief that for the first time in their life they are confirmed in the legitimacy of being who they are and as they are. They say, "My mother, father, teacher, and boss never liked me. It is great for me to find out I am a legitimate type." Of course, all the types have certain negative qualities. Unsympathetic people of a different type pick those things out for emphasis.

The book *People Types and Tiger Stripes*, by Gordon Lawrence, gives some suggestions for determining which type a child is. Once my grandson asked to take the Myers-Briggs test when he saw me scoring some. He was ten years old. Although too young for the test, he is bright, and I let him do it. The test showed that he was not yet more developed in a function with respect to the thinking-feeling or sensation-intuition polarities. But he did test as more judgmental than perceptive. We told his mother about this. It corroborated her observations and was important because all of the others in his family are perceptives. She gave him some responsibility for decisions and they carried out those decisions, which is often hard for perceptives to do without making changes.

Children of different types can be motivated differently. The sensation child needs to be given something specific to do. The intuitive type needs to be inspired. The feeling type will act in order to please someone. A feeling child is motivated for school work, not out of intrinsic interest in the subject matter, but to please a parent or teacher. The thinking child needs to know the reasons for things. In religious education, the thinking type will ask why the different elements of the ritual are practiced. The feeling child probably does not care.

At one Southern California parish 750 families took the Myers-Briggs Indicator. We found that when a child was typologically different from the parents he or she was likely to be treated as the black sheep of the family and picked on. This happens almost inevitably with an introverted intuitive child as there are so few in the population. It can be just as tragic for a sensation type child to have two intuitive parents. If the parents do not understand, they will unreasonably expect too much creativity. One can usually tell if a child takes stories literally, and is therefore the sensation type, or if a child automatically understands them metaphorically, through a developed intuitive function.

Parents can be helped to see the most effective way to motivate a child. It is not effective to scold a child with such things as, "Why don't you clean up your room more often! You never help!" By recognizing the motivation pattern of the type in question, the parent can learn to speak much more appropriately and effectively.

An interesting thing to do with the Myers-Briggs Indicator is for spouses to take the test individually, and then take it again as they think the other partner would answer it. This reveals the areas of misunderstanding between them. One can also take the test on the basis of how one actually functions, as opposed to how one prefers to function. In Florida the Center for the Application of Psychological Types gives workshops for counselors in using and interpreting the indicator.

A group of nuns reported that for community living they found the mixture of perceptive and judgmental types to be the most difficult. The judgmental types wanted everything organized and static. The perceptives wanted nothing organized and everything changeable. The judgmental sisters wanted meals on time, visiting time only once a week for guests, prayer times well defined, rooms cleaned up neatly before the sisters left in the morning. The perceptive-type sisters said their rooms were their own business. If they were working on a project and could not come home without interrupting what they were doing, they wanted dinner later, served buffet-style and kept warm in the oven. They wanted guests anytime except for one community evening. Prayer time was to be whenever it was convenient. We can see the tensions in a community under such conditions of pronounced differences, despite the good intentions of all concerned.

In a family, having two judgmental types together can also be very difficult. Each makes plans and unless they communicate well, the question always arises as to whose plans will be followed. Myers also noted that if two feeling types are together, but with different sets of values, the results can be full of conflict.

Researchers have made some interesting findings about who marries whom, according to typology. Jung's original predictions on the subject were not entirely validated. The research revealed that the least likely combination of traits is marriage between opposite types. The second-least likely combination is partners the same in all categories. There is no right or wrong in this respect: some combinations are a little easier, some a little harder. Every combination needs work to create a successful marriage. The most likely occurrence is that the couple score three categories alike in the profile. The next highest probability is two similarities, then one. When my husband and I originally took the profile, we had only one similarity. Now, after thirty-eight years of marriage, we test alike. People who are very different from their partners have to work constantly on communication. Rarely do words leave the lips of one and hit the ears of the other in the way they were intended.

My husband and I are still developing our communication. In 1976 we went on sabbatical leave. We were flying from Australia to the Holy Land, but had an emergency landing in India. It was our first time there. The temperature was 120 degrees, with severe humidity. We wondered how long we would survive it. We were put in a hotel along with the other passengers and had an opportunity to visit the countryside for five or six days. As we were leaving, I said to my husband, "I'm glad we did not stay any longer in India. I never saw such suffering in my life. If we had stayed longer, I might have felt I would have to stay and serve there." He said, "I had exactly the same feeling." We said no more about it. We assumed we both meant the same sort of thing. Later on we found out differently. I was envisioning setting up a program to get Indians more shade from the oppressive sunlight, with a water system so people would not have to carry heavy water jugs in the heat, along with ample food for the undernourished children. He was imagining teaching them, so that they could broaden their attitudes and lifestyle and take the physical, space-time world seriously. That illustrates the distinct responses of a feeler and a thinker.

People who are very similar have a different communication problem. Sometimes they do not even have to use words, but can communicate unconsciously. Their marriage can become very boring if they do not work at keeping it interesting.

The inferior psychological function, as Jung used the term, is the one opposite the main function. It is the one that is most deeply buried in the unconscious. Spontaneous religious experiences very often, although not always, come through that function. It is the easiest function to stir up, as the ego is paying it the least heed and has the least control over it. The inferior function can also save us when life starts to get dull. At the mid-life crisis, we are often helped when we discover another area of our life that cries out to be developed. Taking care of that gives a new spark of energy. With respect to mystical experience from the inferior function, however, there is nothing one can do to induce it. If such experience comes, it does so by grace. The people who seem to have the highest incidence of extrasensory perception show a profile of being introverted with inward intuition and outward feeling. In other words, their intuition is attuned to the inner world, and they get information that way. As my husband and I travel around the country lecturing we find that intuitive-feeling types are the largest group attracted to our work.

When we reach the point of wanting to develop another function, the best way to go about it is to set ourselves practical tasks involving that function. For example if sensation is to be developed, we can make up our minds to notice the characteristics of every car we pass for a certain period of time, or to note exactly what colors each person is wearing for a day. This can be difficult and boring for an intuitive. But it works. One word of caution though: to the extent that one develops an opposite function, one often loses some from the predominant function because one is not paying it as much attention as before. Energy and attention given to one area are often taken away from another.

If two friends combine opposite strengths it is beneficial to both. When a young Episcopal priest came out of a seminary and first started working with my husband, his wife and I became close friends. I could call her with a question like, "Do you remember a year ago when a certain party came to dinner? What food did I serve then, and what was I wearing?" She invariably knew the answer. I also helped her with my functions in a way that she appreciated. The benefits of both functions were shared.

As for the religious experience of extraverts and introverts, there is an interesting distinction. The extraverts often sense that the Holy Spirit is among us. The introverts feel it is within us. Once, I heard a lecture on this distinction and the following night received a message in a dream that the Holy Spirit is both within and among us!!

Actually very little is known about psychological types. The *Bulletin of Research in Psychological Types* is issued by Mississippi State University. Some of its articles are relevant to the interactions between counselors and their clients based upon types. Yet the field is far from completed. Six years ago there was hardly any printed material to give out at lectures. Occasionally a good article comes out. The journal *Spiritual Life* published one article on "Jung's Typology and Spiritual Life." In summary, it merely said that the spiritual director is well advised to know his or her type as well as that of the clients. Clearly, there is room for much more understanding in this field.

There are prayer forms for the different types. As already mentioned, the sensation types need to start with something concrete and tangible. The intuitives can start with almost anything. But the extraverted intuitives most likely want to use prayer to change the world around them, whereas the introverted intuitives are more interested in the change within themselves. Feeling types appreciate the affective side of religion and prayer. They find expressive gestures very meaningful, such as those of charismatic meetings or liturgical dance. Thinking types want to understand. They often prefer private devotion and writing their own prayers.

On a more mundane level, TWA's *Ambassador* magazine printed an article called "Keeping in Sync with the Other Guy." It was about the experience of American salesmen trying to do business in Japan. They are often unsuccessful because they are usually extraverted sensing types, while most buyers for Japanese industry appear to be intuitive feelers. The American wants to make a quick, efficient, and profitable deal. He or she is invited home by the Japanese buyer to have tea and meet his family. The American just wants to talk about the specifications of the product. But the Japanese needs first to feel a rapport with the seller before being able to develop trust in the product.

The article implied that there are methods to train American salesmen for appropriate behavior in Japanese society. It turns out to be exhausting for the salesmen, but feasible. I have qualms about the authenticity of such an approach. Psychological understanding should not be manipulated in order to sell someone a product that they may ultimately not even want. However, there is an underlying principle that is valid and important for human communication in general. We can make the effort to change our style of functioning at least temporarily so as to be able to communicate with another person who is typologically different. For example, we can talk with children in a language they understand, even though it is not our normal style of speaking. By extension to the church context, this article suggests that we can in fact learn to speak more effectively with fellow spiritual pilgrims whose paths parallel our own.

The Jungian contributions to our understanding of what makes each person unique are subtle, complex, and insightful. They need to be appropriated in a Christian spirit. God created each one of us with love. Jesus incarnated this divine love. If we are to be faithful to the Christian revelation, we need to accept ourselves and one another as we are, and to find within the parameters of our created natures the way to love one another as Jesus Christ loved us.

NOTES

1. The reader may pause a moment, take a piece of paper and write down numbers 1 to 5. After number 1, place the name of the character from the story whom you like the most. 5 will represent the one you liked the least. The other characters should be ranked in between. Then think about the reason for your evaluating them in that way.

Bibliographical Notes: (Much of the material presented in this chapter has come from the following books and articles.)

a. Isabel Briggs Myers wrote a book with Peter B. Myers, entitled *Gifts Differing* published by Consulting Psychologists Press, 577 College Ave. Palo Alto, CA 94306. This is the most helpful book I have found in helping one to understand types.

b. David Kiersey and Marilyn Bates' book *Please Understand Me* is another helpful book on types. It also contains a test called the Kiersey Temperament Sorter that is self-correcting and possible for individuals to self-score.

c. The manual for the Myers-Briggs Type Indicator is published by Educational Testing Service, Princeton, NJ. *Introduction to Type* is published by Consulting Psychologists Press, which gives a brief survey of type theory and the 16 possible type profiles.

d. For those who want to learn more about Jung and about type theory, the Center Point groups are the safest way to make substantial progress. To learn where the group nearest you is located, write:

Center Point
22 Concord Street
Nashua, NH 03060

You can also start your own group through what they give you. They provide tapes and directions on how to organize a group and guidance after that.

e. *People Types and Tiger Stripes,* by Gordon Lawrence, published by the Center for Application of Psychological Types, Inc., is a practical guide to learning styles for teachers and all those who are in close relationship with children.

f. Gerard Fourez in "Prayer and Celebration in the Christian Community," *Worship* 46: 3 (1972) uses Jung's typology with communal worship.

g. Christopher Bryant in *Depth Psychology and Religious Beliefs* discusses Jung's typology as regards private prayer.

h. Marie-Louise von Franz and James Hillman in *Jung's Typology* discuss typology and the inferior functions.

i. Robert A. Repicky, C.S.B., "Jungian Typology and Christian Spirituality," in *Review for Religious* (1981) gives an overview of how typology is necessary for spiritual direction.

Chapter 8

COUNSELING, INDIVIDUATION, AND CONFESSION

Jung was at first reluctant to become involved with religion. He found, however, that the patients he saw often suffered from problems that were essentially religious. When he sent them back to their pastors for help, the pastors did not know what to do. Jung once commented to me, "I had to find out how to help them religiously or I would not have been a healer." I admire in Jung both the sincere humility that made him hesitate to enter the religious domain and the courageous dedication with which he ventured forward once he saw the necessity.

A passion for healing is one of the signs that the spirit moves within. Jung's story reminds me of one of the parables of Jesus. A father asked his two sons to go and labor in the fields. The first son agreed to go but did not actually do it. The second son refused to go, but later changed his mind and went and labored. With respect to the field of religion, Jung was like the second son.

Jung was careful to make distinctions and value judgments. He saw a hierarchy of values in which love was the ultimate. The recognition of a hierarchy of values is consistent with the best in Christian tradition. However, many contemporary Jungians, who follow archetypal psychology, are not so discriminating. They deify the unconscious, without gradations of value. One should be wary of such a point of view, even though it is popular.

Jung was careful to show that the shadow, which can be redeemed, is different from the influence of unintegratable evil, which needs to be avoided or overcome. While the archetypes are operative, we need to deal with them but not be possessed by them. Jung distinguished the physical world from the spiritual world. He differentiated the personal

unconscious from the ego, while also affirming a principle of unity. All of
the distinctions he made are important directives that should not be over-
looked.

The most important problem for personal growth is this: How can we
bring all of ourselves into the fullness of the divine love and how do we
keep ourselves from falling into the disunity propagated by the dark destructive forces? Jung saw four basic elements involved. They are comparable to the steps on the traditional Christian path. Jung called the
process individuation.

The first step is abreaction, in psychological terms, or confession, in
the Christian idiom. It means knowing one's faults and owning them,
usually in the presence of another person. There is little journeying towards individuation without this step. The second step is transference or
love. We grow as we develop relationships and understand them. According to Jesus, our loving one another is the sign that we are following him.
The third step is integration. It involves knowing the outer world and the
people in it along with the inner depths, and trying to function as a unity
inspired by love. It requires a great deal of reflection, education, and
hard work. The goal of wholeness is seldom reached by our own efforts
alone. It is given in the last stage, resolution, that brings us together into
harmony in the divine. Christianity knows this experience as the beatific
vision. Yet the process does not end here. Again and again we go right
back to the beginning. The holier we become, the more we realize the
need to confess, to love, to grow, and to wait. Hopefully, it becomes
easier. The work of the spiritual counselor is to guide others through
these four stages so that they can eventually walk on this path by themselves.

Our individuation is not likely to be a smooth, easy process. Nor is the
guiding of others. Hence, I often find a statement of Mother Teresa's very
helpful. She was asked how she could face the overwhelming odds against
her work in Calcutta, where the people she cared for were just a tiny
fraction of those dying in the streets. She replied, "It is not my job to be
successful. It is only my job to be faithful." Likewise, it is my job to go
with others faithfully through the process of individuation and leave the
results to God.

When we look to Jung to learn how to go about our counseling task,
we find few concrete suggestions. This was one of Jung's shortcomings,
but it is due to his enormous gifts. He was so marvelously intuitive that
he often read people as they stepped into his office. He cared for people
in a natural, spontaneous way. Once, a doctor from the Swiss countryside
brought him a little girl who could not talk. She had not been helped by
any treatment. Jung spent an hour with her, and she left talking. The

doctor asked Jung what he did. Jung looked a little sheepish and said, "Well, I took her on my lap and sang to her."

Listening

Jung was so gifted that he did not realize the need to teach others the essential skill of listening. Many Jungian therapists do not know it, although it is a learnable technique. It requires learning to be quietly present so that others reveal themselves. An intuitive person may have a harder time learning to listen than a sensation type. For an intuitive can often grasp what the other is trying to say and say it for them, thus cutting off the flow of self-revelation from the other person.

In listening, the first thing we need to learn is to withhold facile exclamations and comments that so often shut the other person off. It is hard work for me to refrain for an hour from making a comment when somebody is talking to me. The criterion for successful listening is not that I feel I am doing it correctly, but rather that the other person feels listened to. In the chapter "Psychotherapists or Clergy" in Jung's book *Modern Man in Search of a Soul,* Jung demonstrates that he was certainly a good listener. But the text provides few practical suggestions for a novice wanting to acquire this skill.

I find Carl Rogers' books helpful; we used one of them in a class at St. Luke's Church that was very successful. Our method could be adapted by any parish. After a discussion of the Rogers' book we broke the group of students into pairs. Each pair recorded their work together with a tape recorder. John listened to Caroline speak about a real problem for fifteen minutes. Then they reversed roles. The problems discussed did not have to be major calamities, just real situations. Then the pair would replay their tape and each partner would point out the moments of not feeling listened to. They would bring their tapes and insights back to the class. This simple procedure is effective and much learning can occur.

Some people have a natural ability to listen, which is often related to being able to tolerate ourselves. When we are secure in mature self-knowledge, what another person says is not likely to touch on sore spots that we have not dealt with in ourselves. The more hidden, unfaced parts we have inside, the more we are likely to react to other people's confessions in ways that will interfere with their healing. As a rule, every one of us who is listening to others needs to be listened to in turn. Unless I have someone to listen to me and guide me, I seldom have the right to assume that role for others.

Until a person trusts us enough to share, our guidance is of little value. At ten years of age, my youngest son had spontaneous out-of-the-body experiences. He did not feel free to speak to his mother or me about it. We even sent him to a psychologist but he was smart enough not to say anything about it. Finally he told his mother enough so that we could talk. Then we took him to visit Agnes Sanford. She handled it wonderfully. She was very open to him and soon he was describing his experiences. Then she calmly said, "Well, that is common." She talked about similar experiences and gave him detailed suggestions on how to handle them.

In *The Christian and the Supernatural*, I describe ESP phenomena. If we cannot relate to them comfortably, we can shut people off. For example, an instantaneous unconscious communication can occur. The person may hint at a problem, immediately sense discomfort in the listener, and then avoid the subject that is most important to talk about. We must be able to accept the feelings of other people, or we alienate them.

Jung commented that doctors can accept religious doubts more easily than can clergy:

> As a doctor I can readily admit these doubts. . . . The patient feels my attitude to be one of understanding, while the pastor's hesitation strikes him as a traditional prejudice which estranges them from one another. He asks himself, 'What would the pastor say if I should tell him of the painful details of my sexual disturbances?' He rightly suspects the pastor's moral prejudice is even stronger than his dogmatic bias. In this connection, there is a good story about the American president 'Silent Cal' Coolidge. When he returned home after an absence one Sunday morning his wife asked him where he had been. 'To church,' he replied. 'What did the minister say?' 'He talked about sin.' 'And what did he say about sin?' 'He was against it.'[1]

Does a moralistic condemnation of sin as such really help anybody? What, in fact, is sin? It is anything which keeps us from coming into our unique destiny, into total relationship with love and the risen Christ. This may be different for each person each day. To say one is against sin helps no one. If we can listen to what is troubling another, and bear the burden with that person, then we can help our client or friend to pass through the problem. It is difficult to get over a psychic or spiritual problem, a sin or fear that is hard to face. Usually we cannot do this on our own and we need another to share with us by listening to our pain and confusion.

Jung recognized the difficulties that even doctors might find in trying to listen well:

> It might be supposed that it is easy for the doctors to show understanding in this respect. But people forget that even doctors have moral scruples, and that certain patients' confessions are hard even for doc-

tors to swallow. Yet the patient does not feel himself accepted unless
the worst in him is accepted too.

It may be worse to receive partial acceptance than to be ignored from the
beginning. It can be damaging to a person to give the feeling that we can
listen and then at an intense point show that we cannot deal with the
problem. A flicker in the eye, a slight gesture, a shrug, or a sigh can all
communicate withdrawal of attention.

Helpful listening cannot be created by a verbal declaration of good intentions. Rather, it comes through sincerity, self-understanding, and recognition of our own negativities. As I accept my evil in the love of Christ
and know I can be forgiven for it, I am empowered to work against it in
the knowledge that I can do better. As I face my darkness and know that
I am loved at a deeper level, I can listen to the evil of others in an open
way. If I want to offer guidance to another, I must be in touch with that
person's psychic life, but I cannot do so if I pass judgment. After listening
to a person, it is legitimate for me to point out possible consequences of
his or her actions or attitudes; this is different from passing moral judgment. I abort a relationship if I express my opinions too soon. It does not
matter whether I express the judgments in words or in nonverbal signals.
In either case, they can be felt. Jung suggested that taking the opposite
position and agreeing with the other person can be equally useless and
estranging. We need to accept the facts, whatever they are, and then see
what is appropriate. As Jung said, "Condemnation does not liberate, it
oppresses. I am the oppressor of the person I condemn, not his friend
and fellow sufferer."

I doubt if it is possible for most of us to see and accept ourselves as we
are, unless we can bring ourselves to a center of loving concern. Again
and again I am amazed that when I fall flat on my face and cry out, "Lord,
help," there are the divine arms outstretched to pick me up out of the
pit.

Most people are suffering not because they fail to judge themselves.
Rather, they judge themselves so severely that they cut themselves off
from the love of God. Jung wrote:

> Perhaps this sounds very simple, but simple things are always the most
> difficult. In actual life it requires the greatest discipline to be simple,
> and the acceptance of oneself is the essence of the moral problem and
> the epitome of a whole outlook on life

He knew the New Testament very well:

> That I feed the hungry, that I forgive an insult, that I love my enemy
> in the name of Christ, all these are undoubtedly great virtues. What I

do to the least of my brethren, that I do unto the Christ. But what if I should discover that the least among them all, the poorest of all the beggars, the most impudent of all the offenders, the very enemy himself—that these are within me and that I myself stand in need of the alms of my own kindness—that I myself am the enemy that must be loved—what then? As a rule, the Christian's attitude is then reversed; there is no longer the question of any love or long-suffering; we say to the brother within us, "Raca," and condemn and rage against ourself. We hide it from the world; we refuse ever to admit ever having met this least among the lowly in ourselves. Had it been God Himself who drew near to us in this despicable form, we should have denied him a thousand times before a single cock had crowed.

Jung concluded that the person who practices modern psychology should look behind the scenes not only at the patients' lives, but more importantly at his or her own. Without doing this, the psychotherapist can become an unconscious fraud. The one who tries it sincerely will admit that to accept oneself in all one's wretchedness is the hardest of tasks, and almost impossible to fulfill.

Owning one's own shadow is abreaction. When I first started in analysis, I needed to find someone who could accept me, listen to all of me, and not be shocked. I always remember Max Zeller saying to me that one purpose of psychotherapy is to give outer acceptance to an individual as a prerequisite to that individual's self-acceptance. One of the purposes of spiritual direction is similarly to give acceptance to people so they can accept themselves and allow Christ to accept them. The church has long known the value of confession.

Confession and Abreaction

The process of abreaction requires first that I find someone with whom I can share all of me. In order to find someone truly qualified, I may have to cry out like the importunate widow and ask repeatedly until I find the right person. God's hand is not foreshortened and he may answer this request in unexpected ways and places.

The first step in confession or abreaction is to share whatever is consciously bothering us. To remember even that, I need to write it down somewhere, preferably in regular journal entries. This is especially necessary for extraverted, thinking-sensation types. A journal can offer us an opportunity to catalogue what is occurring in our life. New problems can be noted and dealt with as they arise. Until I consciously remedy the things that I consciously know are wrong in my life, it is senseless to look at my dreams to find deeper problems. Dreams can show us what is wrong when we don't have any idea of where we are really off the track. The written analysis of what feels wrong in me can be very helpful. The church has often recommended that we make an actual list of failings and then bring them to the confessional. This is wise and practical. Until we reflect on paper, we seldom start on the way of change.

Assessing the appropriateness of emotional reactions is another way of showing what is amiss within. Do I exaggerate emotionally? Do I blow up in anger against someone who has not really injured me? Do I become too easily depressed or have my feelings hurt at slight provocation? Answering such questions honestly can help us to learn to perceive what is going on inside and so help us to control our emotions. This means strengthening our ability to cope with who we are, which is necessary if we are to grow spiritually. It is helpful to most of us to write down our emotional reactions in our journal, otherwise we may forget very easily. The same procedure applies for our mistakes and failures.

Our dreams, fantasies, and visions can also reveal our inner turmoil. A dramatic case of a dream's revealing a hidden truth occurred with a lovely, sympathetic lady who took in stray cats and fed them heavy cream, and who also took in an abandoned young man and raised him. She came to me to tell about a recurrent dream in which she strangled her mother. As it happened, she had had good reasons for wanting to strangle her mother. She was the youngest child and her parents felt, "Now there is somebody who can stay home and take care of us." They did not love her for herself; they used her. It became emotional slavery. She was so brainwashed into her role that she thought that she loved her parents. Her psyche was trying to show her the reality of her anger. She could not see it. A few months later she had a stroke and died. The illness might have been averted had she been able to deal with the pressure of this unacknowledged anger within herself.

When I get to know all about me—my angers, lusts, fears, cowardice, emotional outbursts, immaturity, failure to grow—how can I love me? I doubt if I can, unless I find somebody who can accept me as a human being, for this opens me to the possibility of realizing that the Christ can love me. In *The Other Side of Silence* I give an example of active imagination that visualizes my being accepted by the Christ. I see myself feeling bad and running busily and aimlessly here and there. I come back to my soul room and it is a mess. As I enter the vestibule, I am appalled. It is musty. Inside the room, the radio and television are blaring. I sit down on the sofa and the springs push up through the cushions. I cannot even be comfortable. Broken furniture is in the corner. In the kitchen, dirty dishes are piled high in the sink. Garbage is piled high in one corner and rats are running around. I remember that I have to accept myself if I am going to find Christ.

So my first task is to quiet myself. I go back to the living room, to a place on the sofa where the springs do not annoy me. I turn off the radio and television. As the noise stops, I hear a knocking. My first reaction, of course, is to wonder who is after me now. I go over to the window to see who is trying to come in. No one is there and I wonder if it may be a branch brushing against the window. I go back and remain quiet. I realize that the noise is a persistent, slow, quiet knocking. The way a person knocks at a door reveals a great deal. I gather courage and realize there is a door on the far side of my soul's room that leads to the abyss. The knocking comes from there. I go over, gather up all my courage, and say, "Come in." The voice says, "I cannot. The door is locked and the latch is on the inside." Again I gather my courage and open the door. There before me stands the risen Christ, a crown of thorns on his head, a lantern in hand, a cloak with a gigantic ruby clasp around his shoulder. I am staggered that he should be there. I hesitate. He asks, "Are you going to invite me in?" My first reaction is, "O Lord, I am not worthy; you do not know how messy my life and soul room are." He answers, "Who are you to judge yourself? I died to save you. I love you." I fall down on my knees and say, "Lord, come in."

He crosses the threshold, lifts me up by the hand, and embraces me. We sit at the table and talk into the night. Then I begin to love the one he loves. When I do not allow him to love me and do not accept his judgment of me I am rejecting his sacrifice on the cross for me. I doubt if there can be any healing abreaction or confession except in Jesus Christ's presence. He loves me and picks me up. As we talk together and share in the Eucharist, a thousand legions of angels come and clean my soul room, leaving it spotless. As he departs he says, "Remember, I am always here and always knocking. Lo, I stand at the doorway and knock. Whenever people open to me I will come in and sup with them and bring them transformation."

Jung gives us a therapeutic method and a world view; Christianity gives us a savior who gives these substance. I believe that, more than Jung realized, his attitude of loving kindness and caring came from Christianity. He was told to go out into the field. He said, "No, I will not," but then went forth to bring in the harvest.

NOTES

1. This excerpt and subsequent excerpts in this chapter are from C. G. Jung, *Modern Man in Search of a Soul* (New York: Harcourt, Brace and World, 1955), pp. 233–35.

Chapter 9

LOVE AND TRANSFERENCE

It is almost impossible to learn about oneself without reflection, and reflection is difficult without keeping some kind of written record. As I discussed in *Adventure Inward*, my journal is a spiritual diary that enables me to keep progressing toward integration and holiness. With the aid of the journal, I can thoughtfully consider my own psychological type and clarify my values. I can see how different I am from others and can come to appreciate their uniqueness and values, as well. I can even come to love others who are truly different from me.

While the journal is my tool for self-reflection, my relationships with other people are the playing field upon which I show that I am learning. Psychologists have introduced a word to describe an important aspect of human relations. The word is transference. What it really means is love, being able to be truly moved by love. But because the term love has come to have so many diverse meanings, transference can be a more useful concept.

The sharing of love is at the heart of the Christian spiritual journey. Jesus said that we are his followers insofar as we love one another as he has loved us. At this point much of Eastern religious practice differs from Western spirituality. In the Hindu epic the *Ramayana,* the hero marries a beautiful maiden. They are happy at first but when the hero reaches religious maturity he leaves his wife. Love has no essential role to play in his goal of achieving total detachment. He does not seek to transmute his earthly love into a love of God, but rather, to stand above all emotion.

My friend Robert Johnson (author of *He!* and *She!*) was in India, walking down a street with the Hindu master of the ashram he was visiting. They came upon a beggar. Johnson gave alms to the beggar, but the master criticized him, saying the action could interfere with the beggar's karma. Johnson answered that he gave the money for his own sake, not the beggar's. And this justified the giving of alms in the eyes of the Hindu master.

Rudyard Kipling may have been right in saying that East is East and West is West. In some essentials, there is no bridge. Hinduism surely has some wonderful qualities; many people who were alienated from Christianity found help in Hinduism that eventually led them back to their Christian faith. But in Buddhism and Hinduism there is little emphasis on the love and caring that are essential to the growth process in Christianity.

One of the most interesting insights into being loved is in Charles Williams' novel *All Hallows Eve*. The hero realizes how much he loves his wife only after her death. He cries out, "Why isn't one taught to be loved?" Surely, one has to learn to allow oneself to be loved. For some people, this is harder than to give love. In a fascinating paper, the psychiatrist Dr. Jocelyn recommends that parents should encourage their children to show loving behavior toward them, in addition to giving their love to their children.

We need to define this central word love. M. Scott Peck's excellent book *The Road Less Traveled* reminds us that we cannot go anywhere on the spiritual journey until we first of all learn discipline, or ego development:

> Discipline, it has been suggested, is the means of spiritual evolution. This section will examine what lies in back of discipline—what provides the motive, the energy, for discipline. This force I believe to be love. I am very conscious of the fact that in attempting to examine love we will be beginning to toy with mystery. . . . Love is too large, too deep ever to be truly understood or measured or limited within the framework of words. . . . In an effort to explain it, therefore, love has been divided into various categories: eros, philia, agape; perfect love and imperfect love, and so on. I am presuming however, to give a single definition to love, again with the awareness that it is likely to be in some ways inadequate. I define it thus: the will to extend oneself for the purpose of nurturing one's own or another's spiritual growth."[1]

I would only make one change in that definition: Love is the will to extend oneself for the purpose of nurturing one's own *and* another's spiritual growth. We can seldom nurture another's spiritual growth without nurturing our own; we seldom truly nurture our own spirituality without also nurturing someone else's.

One of the last and finest things that Jung wrote was his great passage on love in *Memories, Dreams, Reflections:*

> At this point the fact forces itself on my attention that beside the field of reflection there is another equally broad if not broader area in which

rational understanding and rational modes of representation find scarcely anything they are able to grasp. This is the realm of Eros. In classical times, when such things were properly understood, Eros was considered a god whose divinity transcended our human limits, and who therefore could neither be comprehended nor represented in any way.

I might, as many before me have attempted to do, venture an approach to this daimon, whose range of activity extends from the endless spaces of the heavens to the dark abysses of hell; but I falter before the task of finding the language which might adequately express the incalculable paradoxes of love. Eros is a *kosmogonos*, a creator and father-mother of all higher consciousness. I sometimes feel that Paul's words— "Though I speak with the tongues of men and of angels and have not love"—might well be the first condition of all cognition and the quintessence of divinity itself. Whatever the learned interpretation may be of the sentence "God is love," the words affirm the *complexio oppositorum* of the Godhead. In my medical experience as well as in my own life I have again and again been faced with the mystery of love, and have never been able to explain what it is. Like Job, I had to "lay my hands on my mouth. I have spoken once, and I will not answer." (Job 40:4–5) Here is the greatest and smallest, the remotest and nearest, the highest and lowest, and we cannot discuss one side of it without also discussing the other. No language is adequate to this paradox. Whatever one can say, no words express the whole. To speak of partial aspects is always too much or too little, for only the whole is meaningful. Love "bears all things" and "endures all things" (1 Cor. 13:7). These words say all there is to be said; nothing can be added to them. For we are in the deepest sense the victims and the instruments of cosmogonic "love." Being a part, man cannot grasp the whole. He is at its mercy. He may assent to it, or rebel against it; but he is always caught up by it and enclosed within it. He is dependent upon it and is sustained by it. Love is his light and his darkness, whose end he cannot see. . . . Man can try to name love, showering upon it all the names at his command, and still he will involve himself in endless self-deceptions. If he possesses a grain of wisdom, he will lay down his arms and name the unknown by the more unknown, *ignotum per ignotius*—that is, by the name of God. That is a confession of his subjection, his imperfection, and his dependence; but at the same time a testimony to his freedom to chose between truth and error.[2]

Jung refers to the reality of God as love, with all the mystery that this implies. And this is basically the message of the incarnation, the crucifixion, and the resurrection, as the unfailing, mysterious love of God for miserable people like you and me becomes one of us, dies for us, and rises again.

I recently heard a statement of Mother Teresa's that speaks to the point. A brash young Catholic reporter asked her, "Are you a saint?" "Yes," she answered, pushing her index finger into his chest, "and so are you." A saint is simply one who lets the love of God be the motivating principle of life, as Mother Teresa does. Saint Catherine of Siena was asked by one of her nuns, "How can I pay God back for all of His goodness to me? How can I give back to God some glory for all His kindness, His love, His mercy, His generosity?" Saint Catherine answered, "It won't do you any good to do any more penances. It won't do you any good to build the great church, because God has the whole world as His sanctuary. It won't do you any good to add any more quiet time in prayer. But I tell you something which you can do to really pay God back for the love He gives you. Find someone as unlovable as you are, and give that person the kind of love that God has given you." When we try this prescription we grow spiritually.

In all spiritual direction, one of the tasks is to make the unlovable person lovable through loving them. Recognizing my limitations, I pray, "Lord, I cannot love them, but maybe you can love them through me." This can be amazingly effective. Love is active, not passive. The proof of the loving is not that I feel warmly toward another, but that the person actually feels loved by me. Love alone can truly open the portals of another soul. When two individuals are in such caring rapport, divine love communes with itself through them. This is the ultimate in Christian mysticism.

Learning to Love

The first step toward the mystical peak is "judge not, lest ye be judged." Jung provides the psychological base of that truth: I cannot get close to anyone else until I stop judging myself so that I no longer find it necessary to judge others.

The second step is to listen. Can anyone feel loved if not listened to? Every Christian church should offer listening classes. Is it any wonder that the growth of vital Christianity progress so slowly? Our faith has not failed; it has not yet been tried.

The third step is to realize that people can be different from ourselves and still be valuable. For example, as we indicated in chapter 7, for an introverted intuitive type like myself to see the value of an extraverted sensory-thinking type requires the full actualization of my Christian charity. Sometimes I catch myself wondering if such people can even be made into Christians. This charity becomes all the more important when people are living together in community.

If we allow ourselves to love we must cope with the problems of sexuality and projection that come quickly into the picture. Many good Christian ministers who thought they could manage one-to-one relationships without getting involved have disappeared with their choir directors. This was a scandal in the early Pentecostal church. One has to recognize that when one loves, the power of sexuality may arise. We need to learn to deal with it. The best way to fall under the assault of sexuality and allow it to turn negative is to pretend that it is not there. In such a case, one is nearly defenseless.

One of the problems of the archetypal psychology that has grown out of Jung is that some of its practitioners act as if anything that feels good is of God. But everything in us may not be of God! Therefore we need to look closely at what happens when two people fall in love.

Sexuality and Love

In every man there is an unconscious femininity, which Jung called the anima. In every woman there is an unconscious masculinity, which Jung called the animus. What happens when a man and woman are in close proximity and sharing deeply with one another? Sometimes something quite strong takes place. All of a sudden the woman takes on an angelic quality in the eyes of her man. All her movements appear gracious, all her words wise, all her actions meaningful. If the woman reciprocally perceives the man, a very powerful emotional magnetism flows between them. The man appears to the woman as handsome, intelligent, and heroic. Anyone counseling other people needs to be aware of this possibility. Such awareness gives one the possibility of dealing with the phenomenon when it happens. The mystery, the problem, is that love, over which we may have little conscious control, is a central healing factor in all psychotherapy, religion, and spiritual direction.

When a man becomes enchanted with a woman in the way described, he is projecting his anima ideal onto her. Likewise, the woman projects her animus ideal onto the man. The individual suddenly thinks, "If only I could be with that person, I would be whole." The wholeness that is needed, however, is an inner integration, as illustrated by the diagram in figure 5.

Closeness with the other person may or may not contribute to that integration, depending on many factors. I can too easily try to substitute closeness to another for the inner work that needs to be accomplished. I am foolish if I think that I am going to become so integrated that I will not continue to project. In the context of counseling, when the client

Figure 5

projects his or her ideal onto the therapist, it is called transference. When the therapist does this onto the client, it is called countertransference. Hilde Kirsch, the magnificent therapist with whom I worked, said to me, "No transference, no therapy." Fear of becoming emotionally involved can impede spiritual growth. Love is the explosive inner dynamic of therapy and relationship. Sexuality in itself is a physical symbol of the desire for wholeness, which is more psychological than physical. In their book *The Pleasure Bond,* Masters and Johnson make the important observation that deeply gratifying sexuality on a continuing basis is possible only for a couple who can truly communicate. Sexual pleasure is, in the last analysis, a function of communication.

Insight into the ways we project onto others the animus or anima ideal enables us to begin to integrate this inner quality. Through projection we find another way to know ourselves. Enduring love seldom occurs when two people are unaware of the source of their strong feelings and jump into an intimacy that is only projection. Fulfilling love is rather a result of a real relatedness between two people who are working toward being integrated within themselves. Only then is a true interpersonal intimacy of full communication possible.

In homosexuality, a more complex variation of the phenomenon of projection and transference occurs. For example, the man takes on a feminine attitude and pushes the masculine into the unconscious. Then he seeks in an outer figure the qualities he is missing, in this case, the masculine ones. In other words, he projects his own missing masculinity onto other males, and desires union with them. The same thing can happen with two women. In *Prophetic Ministry,* I have written at length on this subject.

Projection becomes evil only when it is regarded as a true picture of outer reality. We would probably not learn very much about ourselves were it not for projection. It enables us to see ourselves in the mirror of other people. The person who really inspires me will probably tell me more about myself than about that person. If we follow the lives of people with multiple divorces, we see that they repeatedly marry the same type. When I am counseling someone in a divorce crisis, I usually ask that person to promise to bring the new prospect to see me so I can point out the possibility of repetition of the same old unsuccessful pattern.

While touching is a great method of communication in the proper situation, I caution against touching a person with whom there is a transference or love, particularly in private. Touch can be a sacrament of healing. Dolores Krieger's book *Therapeutic Touch* is a testimony to the therapeutic power of touch, even though written from a nonreligious perspective. Within the counseling situation, where propinquity is part of the situation, one of the ways of keeping things within bounds is to be wary of touch. The counselee must never be used to meet the counselor's needs.

And it is likely that the counselor will have needs; the important thing is to be aware of them. Touch may work well in service of a group, but individual counseling poses greater problems in this area. I am not discounting the positive value of touch, but rather advising awareness of where it can lead. Spiritual friends and directors need to follow the same caution.

Reflecting within our journal can be invaluable when a transference hits us. It is amazing how even very intelligent people can be totally taken over by a transference. A famous example is the great British philosopher John Stuart Mill. He often visited a somewhat frowsy woman in London and claimed that all his philosophical ideas were inspired by her. This instance shows how important the inner feminine can be to a man when he is in touch with it. A marvelous book is available on the subject, *Power in the Helping Profession,* by Adolf Guggenbühl-Craig, the present director of the Jung Institute in Zurich. He has written another excellent book on human intimacy, *Marriage—Dead or Alive.* His basic point is that if we get married to be happy we will probably end up unhappy and divorced. However, if we marry because it is our conscious destiny or salvation we will probably be happy and stay married. Marriage can be viewed as no less than a salvation pathway.

Clergy, doctors, lawyers, and psychologists are sitting ducks for projection. Their roles draw projections from others in a startling way. With the new wave of women clergy it will be interesting to note what kinds of transference patterns will develop. I have already stated that I am careful to limit my sessions with someone until I am sure that, if a transference does occur (transference is not always necessary to successful counseling), it will be probably in a creative pattern rather than a destructive one. Once the transference occurs, I can damage or even destroy someone by breaking it prematurely. Celibate clergy and older men should also be very cautious when they counsel younger women. Transference can be so strong as to keep a woman from developing a real relationship with an eligible younger man. With years of counseling experience, an older man can be warmer and gentler than most younger men. I usually avoid counseling young women and try to refer them to women counselors.

If a transference becomes onerous and I try to break it off, I must be careful. Transference can last for decades. Love can turn into hate, and the person who feels rejected or deceived may seek psychological revenge. Transference is one of the most creative forces in the world. Yet, like dynamite, it needs to be handled with care.

Sarcasm, since it is demeaning and rejecting at the same time, interferes with genuine love or transference. It should never be used in a counseling situation and it is even worse in a family situation, where it can become demonic.

Whenever we wish to grow, we will find that love or transference provides the healing stimulant. In his first epistle, John says, "God is love." He goes on to say that the person who does not love his brother or sister, whom he sees, cannot love God, whom he does not see. This reminds us of Jesus' proclamation that his disciples will be recognized as they love one another as he has loved them.

Love, which is a divine power, is paradoxical in that it can be mischanneled. Those who are sexually promiscuous can short-circuit real relationships, and may never learn how to relate adequately to the opposite sex. Real sexuality should occur only after communication, not as a substitute for it. Sexual experimentation by teenagers is a very dangerous modern phenomenon. Love without sex can promote psychological and spiritual growth once we realize that we need to relate to the contrasexual side within us before we can give the totality of what we are to another person.

The cost of psychological analysis makes it prohibitively expensive for the poor. This is another reason why the church needs to provide spiritual direction. And why should Christians have to go for analysis to a secular person who knows nothing of the church's teaching, particularly on the centrality of love? Yet I believe the person receiving counseling needs to give something in return if the process is to be taken seriously and be truly healing. At St. Luke's, those who came to see me as a counselor usually had to agree to give a tithe of time or money to the church. This actually stimulated the process of transformation.

A difficult problem to deal with is what to do with people who are on the borderline of deep disturbances. Psychotics and neurotics are often attracted to small group meetings, prayer groups, or counseling in a church. We need to be prepared for this possibility. Jung said that a psychotic may have as vivid an experience of the divine as other people but is not able to do anything with it. For that very reason, such people are going to be attracted to a prayer group, particularly if the Spirit is moving in it. But they can disrupt it and spoil it for others. It is necessary to take such people aside and define the limits of behavior in the group. They need to be told firmly that they cannot come unless they stay within the limits. Learning to live within socially acceptable limits can help borderline personalities overcome their essential problems. We use a different set of rules in dealing with such people. The psychotic often needs to be treated like a small child, with love and firmness, otherwise the prayer group will be sabotaged. In counseling, I do not feel called to treat psychotics. I refer these people to my colleagues who have the skills and facilities to help them.

Stages of Life

In *Modern Man in Search of a Soul,* Jung observes that we go through various stages of life. The small child (up to five years old, depending on the individual) does not yet have a real ego. The child moves back and forth between a dreamlike state and reality. Many psychotics have a childish adaptation to reality. In this first stage, the child can be influenced more than in any other period. Intelligent, loving parents and teachers can have a great impact upon them, fostering genuine faith by giving unconditional love. By really showing love to children of that age, we can lay the foundations of faith.

The second period, from about age six to puberty, is the age for which the Catholic church spends most of its resources in parochial education. Yet at this time children are least receptive to people other than their parents. Much of the effort is wasted. It would be better to spend money for Catholic education on the earlier period or on high school. Children in the first two stages should not be encouraged to interpret dreams, but, at the same time, their dreams and fantasies should be accepted and honored.

The third stage is that of adolescence. The teenager is seeking an identity and is very responsive to anyone of either sex who really cares and listens. During this period it is important to give loving attention, to encourage imagination, and to give a reasonable basis for faith. Our psychological understanding can determine our success in sharing our faith. Teenagers need to be treated psychologically as adults, not as children. They can be led when we show an understanding of their turmoil, but seldom can they be pushed.

Adulthood can begin at various times, from age nineteen onward. Sometimes people are slow in assuming adult responsibilities, and some never do. Once, my wife and I were traveling home in our car. A dog ran in front of the car and was hit and injured. We stopped and went to see the dog's owners. A ten-year-old girl was comforting her mother who had fallen apart over the accident. Although the mother was ostensibly the adult in the family, her young daughter was the real adult. Some children are forced to be too mature. Often they need to go back as adults and have a childhood again.

Somewhere about the age of thirty-five, we are shocked by the thought that life is half over and wonder what significance life ultimately has. This is a period of existential questioning when the church can meet a real need. Many people come to this crisis at a much earlier age. The golden age of adulthood, which can begin at any time after we resolve the crisis of middle age, can be a time of great creativity. We see our place in the universe, our meaning and direction, and what God wants us to do. Usually we are at our financial peak and we have fewer outer responsibilities, and so we work at fulfilling our destiny. Some time after seventy, seventy-five, or eighty, old age arrives. It can be a glorious time of reflection and moving out of activity to prepare for the next mutation, if indeed we can envision an afterlife. The church and the spiritual friend can offer much at this time of life.

The tasks appropriate for the spiritual director or counselor differ, depending on the life stage of the seeker. Helping teenagers is especially delicate. They must learn to master sexuality or they will be enslaved by it. They have to find an identity, choose a profession, cope with the demands of school, work, and dating. The spiritual director must therefore be aware of the full range of crucial problems a person is facing at a particular age.

Some people have developed inflated egos. They think they can adequately manage life and the world. Such a soul condition is not merely a block to spiritual progress; it is a dead-end street. What is often termed a nervous breakdown, is more often a realization of our powerlessness, imperfection, and inadequacy—and an inability to accept this reality. Such a person is ready to be helped into the inner world, provided the ego remains intact. It is almost never our task to shatter another's illusions about himself or herself.

There are different approaches to helping a person into the inner world. Contemplation or imageless prayer is not the same as the fantasy journey. They are complementary aspects of the spiritual path. One friend sees the imageless approach as more feminine and the focused imagining as more masculine. Just as we need both elements within us personally, we also need both spiritual approaches. Some people totally ignore the value of images, thinking that total growth can come through imageless contemplation alone. There is a real danger here, as individuals then cut themselves off from the corrective images that arise within the psyche when it is off the track. Saint Theresa of Avila tells of moments of imageless ecstasy, but they last but a short time and *always* need to be balanced with inner pictures and images if we are to come to wholeness. God evidently believed that images were so important that He became incarnate in Jesus Christ. Only so could the Holy One be known.

As we mentioned in a previous chapter many extraverted sensation-type people find their contact with the inner spiritual world largely through outer experiences. The Eucharist is an outer drama that conveys an inner spiritual reality. Indeed, all sacraments do just that. The rosary, so often neglected and belittled in recent years, has deep value and significance for extravert sensation-type people; it combines prayer with touch and meditation. Of course, sacramental practices can be misused, but so can imageless practices.

Drugs and Spiritual Growth

This brings us to the timely subject of drugs and religion. We have our heads buried in the sand if we do not realize that this poses a religious problem. Some 65 percent of our young (and not so young) have used marijuana or stronger substances. If we do not understand what they are doing we may not understand them well enough to touch them religiously. There is one good study of drug use in our culture; it is written by Dr. Andrew Weil, a medical doctor who has worked with government agencies on drug abuse, and it is called *The Natural Mind*. He views marijuana as an "activated placebo" that gives us permission to "turn on"— the drug is effective more through the power of suggestion than chemically. Weil suggests that we have an instinctive need to relate to the spiritual dimension, and marijuana offers a way of pop meditation. Unless the church can understand that there is a spiritual dimension and offer a spiritually more significant method of bringing these people into contact with that reality, it will have little impact upon them. I am quite certain that the Eucharist in the first centuries of the church's life provided just such a spiritual encounter. One of the great values of the charismatic movement is that it offers experience, not just doctrine and words.

Weil suggests that one of the reasons so many young people are using drugs is that our society offers very few, if any, legitimate institutions that provide an acceptable way to attain altered states of consciousness. The undergraduates whom I taught at Notre Dame used drugs at the rate of the national average and they agreed that this was their basic reason for doing so. One student in a class on religious experience wrote a paper at the conclusion of the course in which he said that he had not known that there was any way other than LSD to obtain a depth experience. He had then learned that this was the very purpose of the meditation advocated by the church since its inception. This admission came from a student who had sixteen years of formal church education.

Drugs are dangerous. They take a person into the unconscious. They remove the ego stopper of consciousness and they do it without control, history, or tradition to provide guidance. F. Bruce Lamb's *The Wizard of the Upper Amazon* points out that among the South American natives who use hallucinogenic drugs for religious purposes, there is a strict taboo against using them outside of the ritualistic worshipping context. While drugs can open us up, they may open us up to the darkness known as the bad trip. This is a real risk. Another danger is that people with unstable personalities can be split apart by even the mildest hallucinogenic drugs and come together only with the greatest difficulty.

Final Comments

Individuation is not the same as holiness; it is the name given by Jung to the process of spiritual growth which can lead to holiness.

Feelings should never be equated with actions. When depth psychologists tell us that most of us have innate homosexual feelings, they are not suggesting that these need to be acted out. The same is true of heterosexual transference feelings within the counseling session. For male counselors, being in touch with the feminine hardly means that one should act out physically. But it can bring us into touch with the unconscious through the anima and may even spur us on to spiritual growth.

Reading the newspapers leads one to think that evil is on the increase. How can we reconcile our sense of evil with our religious faith? Faith does not lead us to deny these facts. Rather, faith is the conviction that at the very heart of the universe, evil is already defeated. If I have faith, I am moving with the grain of the universe. Eventually, love and caring will be justified as the way of eternity. Mysteriously, people with that kind of conviction and action help defeat the evil rampant in our society.

Psychological depression and the dark night of the soul also need to be distinguished. The former condition can be caused by severe psychological trauma of one kind or another. The dark night of the soul occurs when there is an opening in the wall between the ego and the depths of the soul. As those depths become visible, they appear dizzying and dark, but they can be truly the passageway to growth. Many people on the spiritual journey encounter this state. It requires dealing with our own inner darkness, with evil, with our murderer, with the idiot within. Faith can help carry us through to our divine destination, but we often need skilled guides on that path.

NOTES

1. M. Scott Peck, *The Road Less Traveled: The Psychology of Spiritual Growth* (New York: Simon & Schuster, 1978), p. 81.

2. C. G. Jung, *Memories, Dreams, Reflections* (New York: Pantheon Books, 1963), pp. 353ff.

Chapter 10

MOVING TOWARD INTEGRATION

We have seen that individuation takes place in stages. The first stage is abreaction or confession—finding out what we are really like in order to transform what needs changing. It is a difficult and painful process. Next comes transference—the capacity to become so close to others that the divine can be manifested in and through the relationship. If we are truly loving or caring enough, we can see into the depth of another human being and help that person feel totally accepted, or we can be on the receiving side.

Freud, however, used the word transference differently. For him it meant that the patient transferred onto the therapist the parent image. This enabled the two to work together. The ending of the transference indicated the completion of therapy. My use of the term transference is clearly distinct from Freud's. I mean that the client and I see something very positive in each other. This enables counselees to share all of their being with me. It promotes full abreaction and gives a sense of love or care.

The movie *The Elephant Man* illustrates many psychological truths, in particular the healing potential of transference. John Merrick was a grotesquely deformed individual living in England several generations ago. A doctor found him being exhibited in a sideshow. The doctor saw past the externals to the sensitive soul within and took Merrick to a place of shelter and care. Merrick's artistic skill in making architectural models flourished in this setting. From Jung's point of view, the doctor accepted and loved the freak in himself, and Merrick loved the beautiful, strong, creative man hidden within himself.

Transference can be expressed negatively as well as positively. In some marriages, the couple do nothing but fight, yet they remain together. One wonders why. They seem attracted to each other's anger and hostility. Occasionally in a counseling relationship, the client seems to act out an intense dislike for the counselor, fighting verbally with him or her and testing the counselor in every way. Yet this can be creative, as it enables the person to deal with the angers and hostilities that otherwise would not be admitted. Because transference makes us vulnerable to one another, it is powerful. Therefore it can be misused. I am mistaken if I simply cut off a transference without discussing the issue with the other person. I am equally mistaken if I allow someone to live in dependency on the transference rather than prodding them to use it as a creative means of inner integration. Properly managed, a transference can help with healing when we see through the other person to the divine which actually dwells in each of us. Seeing the divine calls forth admiration, reverence, and respect. We realize that we can never use such a person as an object. We are here on earth to relate to each other in equality and mutually accorded dignity. We can in this way experience the divine mystery of love.

Out of a genuine relationship may come transformation of both partners, the counselor and the client. Max Zeller once told me that in every good counseling hour, he gained more than his patients did. This surely is true for the spiritual director. As Jesus indicated, if we do not love our neighbor, we are not allowing the love of God to pass through us to the other person. What greater benefit could there be for us than to let the love of God thus flow through us for the healing of our neighbor.

The next stage of the individuation process is integration—growing more steadfast in our insight and its actualization. This cannot be understood merely by reading about it. Like the Christian gospel, it is learned through practice and experience, not through rational argument. Jung was almost scornful of those who thought they could find out about the nature of the inner life by reading about it. This is tantamount to thinking one can learn about heart disease in human beings without listening to hearts. The psyche is as palpable a reality as the human heart or the chair in front of me. The only way I can come to know the soul is to work in the laboratory of my own inner being. I accomplish this through prayer, listening to my dreams, active imagination, journal keeping, and other practices. In my own inner journey, I have learned many lessons about integration.

Milestones Along the Way

My first lesson was that unless I had time alone each day, I betrayed myself. Unless I took time to work with my soul, I betrayed both my soul and the Christ who loved me. No one in the church or seminary ever suggested to me that at least a half hour a day should be consecrated to my inner reflecting and devotional practice. Nor was I advised that every week or so I needed two or three hours for spiritual housecleaning. This was not suggested most likely because the soul was regarded as a rationality alone, as a vaporous substance without much reality. I was, supposedly, only intellect. But depth psychology helped me see and deal with those parts of me beyond the rational. I learned that to avoid neurosis I needed these regular times alone.

A minister on the verge of a nervous breakdown once came to Jung for help. The man complained that he was working fourteen hours a day, that he could not sleep at night, and that he would soon collapse. Jung listened and then asked, "Do you want to get better?" The minister answered, "Yes." Jung said, "Well, I have a simple prescription for you. Go home tonight and stop work at suppertime. Tomorrow morning, get up, go to work, spend only 8 hours in ministering, and come home to spend the evening entirely by yourself. Do the same thing the next day. The following morning come back to see me." The minister expected a fancier prescription than this but said he would try it. When he came back to Jung two days later, he said the prescription had not worked and he felt as bad as ever. Jung asked the minister what he had done. The man answered, "I went home the first night and told my wife I wanted to be alone. I went into my study, closed the door, and sat down in a big leather chair. I was quiet for a moment and then I noticed a book by Hermann Hesse. I picked it up and read it. After a while I went over to my piano and played some Chopin." The next night the minister spent in a similar way, reading Thomas Mann and playing Mozart. His wife expressed doubt that such treatment would be effective. Jung heard the report and said, "You did not get the point. I did not want you to be with Hesse and Thomas Mann, with Chopin and Mozart. I wanted you all alone by yourself." The minister replied, "But I cannot think of any worse company." Jung replied, "Yet you inflict it fourteen hours a day on other people." This story illustrates the first lesson I learned: if I do not take some time alone with myself, I have no right to be with other people.

The second thing I learned was that my inner life needed to be disciplined. This message came to me in a dream. I saw myself as a student in a military academy. Having once taught in a military academy, I knew it was a fate worse than death to be there as a student. What on earth was the dream telling me? The implication was clear. I had to get some discipline into my life, to schedule times for eating, recreation, prayer, study, family life, friendship, preparing sermons, parish business. Without a disciplined outer life, I would make little progress.

My third insight was an enormous one. Although I had thought of myself as quite intelligent, I had fallen into a pit and I could think of no way out. I was immobilized. Then a series of dreams gave me new ways of looking at things that enabled me to turn my life around and to begin to live again.

The first dream was a simple one: it was merely the visual image of a pink peach pit. I took the dream on my first visit to Max Zeller. He asked me to associate to it. My association to peach was Georgia, which reminded me of an aspect of my life that I had never discussed with anyone and that was burning to be talked about. How greatly my anxiety diminished when I talked about this hidden area of my life.

I realized that something in me was wiser than my consciousness and was able to prod me toward health and renewal. The dream went right to the heart of a major problem of mine. A peach pit is a seed teeming with new life. Planted in the ground it dies in that form and a new tree rises out of it, a tree that bears fruit. I realized that my inner agony could become fruitful. Often a first dream, technically called the initial dream, predicts the course of the inner journey, and I was encouraged. On another level, the dream told me that I could let my old attitudes die and that something new and creative would emerge. I began to understand with what great wisdom my dreams could speak, once I learned their language.

The dream of the peach pit helped me solve a paradox. I had held two contradictory statements to be expressive of truth. According to the first, I cannot be real to anyone else unless I am first real to myself and take control of my life. According to the second, which is Jesus' admonition in John 12:24, "The man who loves his life will lose it; the man who hates his life in this world will keep it for eternal life." The peach-pit dream resolved the paradox for me. In the verse just before the admonition, Jesus said, "Unless the seed falls to the ground and dies, new life cannot come." At that point in my life I had to let go of the seed that was my attitude that I could run my own life by myself. I had to give up my pretensions of being adequate to every situation. This dream was given to me by a wiser spirit than my own. I realized that my ego had to give way to a new center. In coming to this new center, I truly become real to myself. For it is only in that center, beyond the ego, that all of me can be accepted and brought into harmony with the divine spirit. The peach pit symbolized the resolution of the paradox. It also implied the necessity of first developing an ego before being able to give it away. A person who never had an ego is in no position to give up his or her life and can fall into a dangerous kind of immature religion. So my first dream enabled me to deal with my personal unconscious and taught me about death and resurrection.

Many years later I had a terrifying dream. I was in a truck going backwards down a steep hill. I put my foot on the brakes, and they did not work. I awoke in a cold sweat and realized that I had to change my life. As I reflected on the dream, I realized I was driving myself too hard. The truck is a vehicle dedicated to work and I had lost control of it. I had to cut down the amount of time I was on the road. Although I was trying to listen to God every day, only that dream could get through my stubbornness.

Shortly after I made that decision to change my lifestyle, I had one of my most numinous dreams. I awoke transfixed. I was pierced by a beam of light that I knew was the presence of God. I fell to the ground feeling unworthy, unclean, and terribly aware of all my mistakes and failures. Then I felt a hand reaching down to mine. The beam of light was transformed into a human being who lifted me to my feet and embraced me. He remained with me and when I went to introduce this person to some friends, I realized that I did not know his name. So I turned to him and asked his name. He said it was Hardly Visible. Time and again when I come into a dead-end street I am guided onward by my dreams. What confirmation this dream gave me!

My next lesson was like a new revelation to me, that fairy tales and myths were exactly like dreams, but they were the dreams of a whole people, not just of an individual. The spiritual dimension revealed itself in this way. The myths that affected me as an individual were describing a part of my inner life just as a dream would do. Needless to say, this had never been taught in the seminary.

I found that when I became very quiet and listened and looked within, images arose from my unconscious and spun themselves into stories. While awake, through quiet and imagination I could enter the same realm as in dreams and these fantasies revealed my inner depths and the spiritual dimensions beyond me. Since I was conscious in the process, I could even nudge the action and change it if it were negative. This practice had an advantage over the sleeping dream. This use of the imagination, though, has no more value than a dream when it is not understood. When I need to confront the inner stories, I do so through active imagination. When I begin to direct the drama unfolding within my soul, I can sometimes change my personality and even at times the world around me. Truly effective intercession works in this way.

Another of the lessons I learned was that psychic events can have physical effects, just as physical events can have psychic effects. This is the truth behind healing and other gifts of the Spirit. Hence, I began to understand why not a word was said about the charismata during my years in the seminary. They did not fit the space-time world view of those teaching there. As I comprehended the world view of depth psychology, the cases of extrasensory perception among the apostles became more understandable, as did Jesus' foreknowing his death, his sending the disciples out to find the man with the jar on his head, or sending them ahead to get the donkey. Jesus' healings also made sense. Within my new framework of understanding, these were natural events.

My next discovery was that artistic works reveal the soul of their creator. The writings or drawings of confused people often reveal their problems. A sick person's drawings are of his or her soul. One of the most interesting personality tests is based on some simple drawings. The subject is given three pieces of paper. The instruction for the first piece is to 'draw a person.' For a second piece, the subject is asked to draw a person of the opposite sex from the first drawing. The third picture is a drawing of a family. In most cases, this simple procedure reveals a person's relations to mother, father, masculinity, and femininity, as well as the subject's place in the family. We draw what is in our souls. When we are creative, we express our depths: the only difference between the little story I wrote for a school theme and great literature is that the latter captures the imagination of a whole people and reflects a whole society. One example is *The Strange Case of Dr. Jekyll and Mr. Hyde* by Robert Louis Stevenson. Why did this book touch Victorian England so deeply? It is clear that the story mirrored the society. On the surface there were elegant tea parties and cultural finery. Underneath, there were the poor, child labor, an arrogant foreign policy, and fortunes built from the slave trade. Because it revealed the rottenness beneath the sugar coating of the social graces, the book gripped people. Similarly, why did Emily Brontë's *Wuthering Heights* have such dramatic appeal? The character of Heathcliffe personified the author's own murderous animus destroying her from within. It was a common problem for Victorian women. This theme gives the book its authenticity and perennial appeal to readers.

One of the lessons that was most difficult for me to learn is the fact that we cannot go on the inner journey without suffering. Jung discusses this many times. He knew the way of the cross and described it in psychological terms. In this light, the crucifixion becomes even more meaningful. As we go the inner path there are necessary sacrifices, old skins to slough off before new ones can emerge, seeds to cast into the ground so that new plants can grow. The shamans of nearly every culture have spoken of dismemberment and resurrection.

During the stage of integration, I also learned to use a journal in greater and greater depth. My journal helped me to talk to the Lord, to develop my active imagination, to reflect upon my inner life. With it I learned that the events of my outer life affect my inner life, especially as concerns my morality. When I break my moral code, I affect my body and psyche.

Jung told the story of a very neurotic young man who came to see him. The fellow made a careful analysis of his life. Jung had never seen a better one, in fact. But the analysis did not clear up the neurosis. Jung noted that the man spent part of his summers up in the Alps and his winters in southern Switzerland. This is a very pleasant arrangement, but the young man did not have much money. Consequently, Jung asked him how he got the money to do this. He answered, "Oh, there is an older teacher down there. I provide for her physical necessities, and she gives me the money to do what I want." Here was the source of the neurosis. One usually cannot live against one's moral code without becoming psychologically ill. Often physical illness follows close behind. What I do in my outer life has consequences for my inner life.

My next insight had to do with the centrality of love. I learned that I have to allow love to permeate my life entirely. Love must become a way of life. If I mistreat people close to me, any pretenses I have about being loved will not be taken seriously. In this connection, Jung once met a very holy man who impressed him so much that he felt he might have to change his ways and adopt that religious attitude. Then he met the man's wife, upon whom the ostensibly holy man projected most of his shadow. Jung realized that the man's holiness was a facade. Unless we are continually working on expanding our love, we will not be adequate as directors of conscience or as spiritual friends. The first place for the realization of my love is within my own family. If I do not love my family, my relations with my clients in counseling or spiritual direction are fraudulent. Then I need to look at how I treat my acquaintances, the clerk at the store, the bus driver. Further, how do I treat my enemy? Do I reach out to the stranger? Unless my love extends in all these directions, it will not be a channel for divine love. I have discussed this aspect of life in depth in my book *Caring*.

I then began to realize that I needed to read the writings of the saints and mystics. I could learn about holiness only from holy people. To fathom the depths, heights, and possibilities of inner life, we constantly need to read the best examples of it. Of course, the Bible is one of the best resources. But we need other reading as well.

That each person has an individual destiny came as a new insight. This is what individuation means. Each of us has our own individual way to go. This does not mean there are no objective moral values. Rather, it means that we each use these moral values in an individual way. What are some of the perennial values? Jesus, as an expression of love, tells us that the nature of the universe is love. When I am not genuinely loving in the way Jesus expressed it, I am going away from the center of reality and against the grain of the universe. The second abiding value is that my actions always be dedicated as much as possible to the purpose of genuinely showing love to other people. I may never use another person for my private gain or satisfaction.

There is wisdom in the church's prohibitions regarding sexuality. During the Middle Ages, couples were first betrothed, then lived as man and wife, and finally came back for the actual marriage when they had children. But the relationship was regarded as legitimate from the beginning. In the wedding ceremony, the man and woman getting married are the priest and priestess. The official priest of the church is really only a witness. Marriage is a sacrament. A couple should be deeply conscious that this union is sacred in that from it new life may spring. Sexuality outside of commitment can cause damage. Sex is not a plaything or a toy. When we take control over others we violate love just as when we use dependence for selfish ends. While these values are abiding, each person will relate to them in a unique way. Each of us has a unique destiny.

One other lesson from my Jungian involvement is one that I should have learned in seminary but did not; it is that life goes on after the death of the physical body. Jung frequently affirmed that he found nothing in the psyche to indicate that the physical death of a person marks the end of that person's life. My book *Afterlife* shows why so few Christians have convictions on this subject.

My debt to Jung in providing the "from which" and the "how" is incalculable, but there were certain things that my Jungian friends did not provide. First of all they did not teach me commitment to a loving savior upon whom I could call at all times. Had I not had my own theological and religious background I might have been at sea without a compass.

Jung and his followers pointed out that myth is a pattern of reality that can be expressed either through imagination or through history. But without my religious background I would not have received from them the suggestion that the risen Christ might be the ultimate expression of mythology. They did not see their task as that of providing any specific goals for the journey. But those with whom I worked never discouragee my use of the Christ symbol and Jung even calls attention to its centrality in his *Answer to Job*.

One finds a certain fatalism in Jung and some of his followers. There is little or no missionary zeal. When we consider the psychological naiveté of many missionaries who try to force their ideas upon others, we can understand Jung's resistance and reluctance. If, however, our desire is not to bring others around to our ideas, but rather consciously to share with others the gifts and graces we have been given—the Good News that has saved us—there is a place for this sharing. However, we need to be careful when we think we have something of value to share.

Jung said to me: "I am not a prophet; I am a medical doctor. It is not my business to bring people salvation, but healing. If I were to try to preach I would be getting out of my role." We should take Jung at his word and make use of his legacy within the limits he set for it. To the living of our own deep Christian faith, Jung's ideas can contribute a vision of the depth and plasticity of the human soul, its bridgelike character as it spans the gulf between the physical and spiritual world, and many practical methods by which the soul can be transformed, renewed, and reborn in this life and in the one beyond.

For the extraverted type of person many of the basic lessons we have just outlined may have to be learned through other means. As suggested earlier, the daily Eucharist can be very helpful. I also recommend a prayer corner or shrine somewhere in the house as a constant reminder of faith. It can have a crucifix, candles, statues of a favorite saint or two, or an icon. Simply going and sitting before this place can do something for the extravert. Having religious symbols in every room can also be helpful. Certainly the shrine should not be closed off when there is a cocktail party. Wearing a cross is another possibility. I carry a rosary in my pocket. Even though I am basically an introverted intuitive, just reaching in and feeling the corpus on the cross brings me back to thoughts of the source of my ultimate help.

Another thing the extravert can do is to act out a Biblical story. One of the most profound experiences in my life was at Schlöss Carheim in Bavaria. There was a class on symbolism that finished with role playing the story of the prodigal son. Each part was played: the elder brother, the father, the prostitute, the pigs. At the banquet scene, the doors of the hallway were opened, tables laden with fruit, wine and bread were brought in and we celebrated the Eucharist.

Similarly, the extravert can draw pictures of the Bible stories, make clay sculptures, perform plays. Small prayer groups can be tremendously helpful. Working around the church should be considered: an extravert might have a religious experience putting up a new church roof, or preparing and serving a church dinner. These can be acts of Christian sacrificial service.

We have spoken of the need for discipline to make order in our outer and inner life, but how do we encourage it? Most of us find that if we try to impose discipline by our will power alone, we fail. We need the inspiration of a loving person who shows us the value of what we are trying to do, who supports us with love and prayer. Christian communities help in this. I wish more Christian communities offered the sort of group support that is found in Alcoholics Anonymous. People who cannot stop drinking go to be with a group of people who were themselves alcoholics and who say, "I support you unconditionally, even if you get drunk." With this kind of help many are empowered to stop drinking. Likewise, the church needs to be a fellowship of nonpracticing sinners who offer unconditional love of this kind.

Yet, while affirming the person, we need to deal with any unredeemed aspects of the personality. When I listen to a person express a deep doubt or fear about some facet within, I never say, "Oh, but that is all right!" Rather, I need to explore this with the person. I affirm the struggle in that soul and give methods of coping with the problem but I do not act as if the problem itself should be affirmed as an acceptable aspect of life. If a person is unaware of these inner dynamics, I point them out. It is compatible with my love to tell someone that an unnoticed feature of his or her soul is causing trouble. Once, a client was talking to me very deeply about personal visions and an intense spiritual experience. I asked, "But, what are you doing in your personal relationships? Such an involvement can be a substitute for personal relationships." Some of my counselees used to call my office a torture chamber. Yet, all I did was to give them an opportunity to look at whatever was unredeemed in them and then help them deal with it. Many people cannot face their darkness until they have someone to face it with them, one who can realize the horror they feel and help them overcome it. Strangely though, most people feel guilty for the wrong things. Often people feel they are wicked because of relatively minor problems. When they can recognize and confess the truly unredeemed qualities, transformation becomes possible.

Chapter 11

DREAMS AND THE SPIRITUAL WAY

Jung gives us tools whereby we can step back into the mentality of the early church and appropriate the power that was there. But he does not do the integrating for us, even though his world view is fundamentally the same as that of Jesus and the early church fathers.

It came as a revelation to me that in a dream something of the wisdom of the beyond could be speaking to my soul. This staggered me. It meant that there was a way for me to listen to the voice of God, even though Jung did not call it that. Through dreams, some deep inner reality that is greater than my psyche is trying to help me toward my destiny. When I realized this I exclaimed, "My heavens, God speaks in dreams." I wondered what kind of freak this made me in the context of the Christian church. Although I knew that there were a few dreams mentioned in the Bible, I was convinced by the liberal tradition that these belonged to another age and did not apply to us now. In three years of seminary I never once heard that I could expect God to speak to me. Hence, I decided to find out what the Christian tradition really said on this subject of dreams and spent ten years finding out. The results were surprising.

First, I read the Bible from cover to cover. I noted every dream. In the Old Testament, dreams and visions seemed indistinguishable. In the New Testament, Paul's vision of the night was the crucial occurrence that sent him to Europe. Every major movement of growth and transformation reported in the Book of Acts was based on a vision, a prophecy, or a dream. Then I read the ancient Greeks. I learned that the Greeks were even more involved with the unconscious than were the Hebrews. I began to wonder about the origin of the belief that God speaks through dreams. I began my research into the question by buying the thirty or so volumes of the writings of the ante-Nicene and post-Nicene fathers. I memorized the New Testament passages that talk about dreams and looked up the comments the church fathers made on these passages. I found very rich material. Yet the histories of the church fathers that I had read in seminary never mentioned dreams. Nor did the indexes of those large volumes I bought. Liberal Christianity nicely screened all that out.

I shared my discoveries in my book, *God, Dreams and Revelation*. Remarkably, every church father, East and West, believed that the dream was a primary way in which God is revealed to human beings. In Western thought, dreams were first rejected as insignificant nonsense by Aristotle but his rationalism only became influential in the Western church in late medieval times. The Greek Orthodox church was never touched by this stream of thought. Consequently, dreams are still highly regarded there, as in the Russian and other Orthodox churches. In the West though, the lid was closed on the space-time box and people were trapped inside, believing that our only valid experience came through the five senses. Therefore, dreams were dismissed except by those on the fringes of society.

In order to entertain the possibility that God speaks through dreams, we need a theoretical framework supportive of that view. Once we see that the world view we have just provided is similar to the early church, we realize that we are not out of step with the church. In Western church history, only the period from 1400 to 1980 denies the significance of dreams. This is not a time of conspicuous vitality in Chistian life and thought. There were religious wars, bigotry, state churches, persecution of Jews, and figures like Cardinal Richelieu and Henry VIII. I feel ashamed to see how little of the love of Jesus Christ is reflected in most churches, in ecclesiastical hierarchies, and in religious orders. In fact, for fifteen years I have been on the board of directors of a corporation that has treated its employees better than most religious institutions that I know. We must find such love in all levels of the church's life if we are to convert the world.

When the church was most vital it acted in love and saw the dream as evidence of God's love. This church conquered the ancient world by outliving, outdying, outloving and outthinking all rival orientations. Without the help of Jung, I probably would not have a framework for understanding what the early church fathers were talking about. We cannot avoid facing that they affirmed the existence of the angelic and the demonic and that they believed that dreams were one of the best revealers of this other reality.

Interpreting the Dream

How do we listen to our dreams and help others with theirs if no specialists are available to help us? It is not impossible, but it takes desire, dedication, and hard work.

The first step is to begin to write down and reflect on our own dreams, to interpret them as well as we can, to find a sympathetic friend willing to listen and help us in the interpretation. This friend is preferably intuitive, a believer in the ongoing creativity of the Spirit, and someone who knows how to listen meditatively.

The second essential in listening to dreams is to realize that the various characters, whether living, dead, or mythological, probably refer to different aspects of our psychic depths and not to outer circumstances and people. We should always first look at the dream characters as portraying a part of the dreamer. Most of the time this approach will prove valid.

Although dreams comment on outer events, only a tiny fraction of them give data we could not get from the five senses. Among dreams with an extrasensory perception element may be precognitive, clairvoyant, or telepathic ones. They may look ahead into the future, tell about what is happening at the same time in a different place, or pass on a message from another mind. One reason these rare dreams are attributed so much importance is that they are the ones that shock us into realizing how significant strange dreams can be; we remember them and forget the others. Being rather compulsive, I have kept a careful record of my dreams for the past thirty-four years; they probably number 30,000, of which no more than 20 are basically ESP dreams. One never knows whether a dream is prophetic until it is confirmed by an outer event. It is nonsense to suggest that all dreams predict future events. The purpose of dreams is to reveal, correct, compensate, and direct, and *very* rarely to predict.

Some dreams do have a numinous quality, however. One was sent to me by a woman who could not find anyone to listen to her seriously. Her minister suggested she write to me. She dreamt of her son, Michael, who had recently died in a car accident. Here is her description:

> On August 15, 1978, I had a dream. It was more than a dream. I wrote it down as soon as I awoke.
>
> This happened first: A picture of Mike kept flashing or pulsating. He was sitting on something low, left hand or fist under his chin, legs apart and bent, feet flat on the floor, hair down over his forehead, smiling at me and very neat and clean. In this picture he had on his blue plaid cowboy shirt and blue corduroy pants.
>
> "This is the second picture, or happening: I was standing at the sink washing dishes, I looked up and saw Mike sitting or standing by the

pool table, and I said, "Oh, Michael." He had on his red plaid flannel shirt and blue jeans. I walked over to the other side of the pool table and he disappeared. Then he reappeared sitting on the side of the pool table about a foot from me doing one of his trick shots. I put out my arms and he fell toward me and said, "Oh, Mom, someone cut off my breath." Before he fell into my arms he disappeared, and I was just standing there. At first when he first saw me he was happy, then when he said, "Oh Mom, someone cut off my breath," his face was unhappy, like he was going to cry. It was all so real. I can remember thinking that I didn't even get to touch or feel him.

As I was coming out of this dream, I was saying, "Dick, Dick, I've just seen Michael," and I proceeded to tell my husband of my dream. We got out of bed and I wrote this all down. Then I asked my husband what shirt Mike had on when he left the house that morning, and he said, "a yellow T-shirt." So I asked him if he would get the box of clothing down from the attic; we went through the clothes and found the yellow T-shirt, but the red flannel shirt was gone, so Mike must have changed shirts before he left.

After my husband left for work, my daughter was still sleeping and I was trying to work in the kitchen (thinking about all of this) when I noticed the atmosphere in the kitchen and the pool room was so electrifying. It is so hard to put into words how it felt. I felt a little uncomfortable or frightened.

I called our pastor in Illinois and told him about my dream and everything that had happened. He sent me your address and I decided to write to you.

Since my son died, I have prayed and prayed to see him just one more time to make sure he is all right. I think this was my one more time.

This is a perfect example of a numinous dream. Such a dream may happen only once or twice in a lifetime. A few people have them more often. Usually, they are troubling. Whenever someone tells us such a dream, we should listen reverently. We do not have to comment, but we can give them the comfort of taking it seriously. It may well have been God who gave this woman an answer to her prayer that she see him one more time. The dream also suggested that if she held on to him, she might impede his soul's progress. A counselor in the materialist box is at a loss before such a dream. Saying nothing gives the dreamer the impression that we doubt what is being said. Speaking negatively conveys the counselor's scepticism. But it is really important for a person who has had such an experience of a close relative or friend to be taken seriously.

Dreams are neither good nor bad. I am annoyed when I hear people say, "I had a good dream last night," or the opposite. What we call a bad dream is most often a warning about a situation we need to confront. A so-called good dream points out a possibility in need of actualization. The quality of a dream is not measured by what it presents, but by what we do with it. The dream does not often predict the future or reveal inevitable destiny. It gives a situation to which we can react so that we can be transformed and grow. Much is lost when people say, "I had a wonderful dream last night; it felt so good," and do nothing. Unless we take steps to actualize that "good" dream we do not realize our potential in the spirit.

Here is an example of actualization. It is a beautiful dream written by a middle-aged woman who had a hard life and is the mother of an autistic child:

> I was standing in an opening in the woods. The sun was shining, and I was happy to be among the trees. A stranger came toward me carrying something in his arms. He said to me, "This is the rarest dog in all the world. It is a precious gift for you." He set the puppy on the ground, and I thought it was a perfectly ordinary scruffy brown puppy. But I wanted him, and I loved him immediately. The stranger left and I played for a long time. Then we lay down together to rest. I slept. When I awoke there was no puppy. Instead there stood an enormous elegant copper-colored dog with beautiful fur waving to the ground. The ends of his fur were all tipped with gold and there was a golden reflection all about him. I knew he would remain standing there until I really saw him with my soul as well as my eyes. There were no words but there was total communication between us. After a time he was gone. I looked around for him, but suddenly I knew he was gone, but not gone, for the moment I saw him he became a part of me.

She knew she must do something in response to the dream and so she wrote a poem about her experience, about its numinous quality, about its meaning. She began to actualize the experience.

Our dreams are marvelously tailored to our individual needs. She liked animals very much. The dreamer within brought her into a religious experience with Christ through this gift of a dog. If she had simply said, "Oh, nice dream!" and had done nothing with it she would not have been deeply touched and transformed.

A story is told about Pastor Niemuller. After being freed from prison at the end of World War II, Niemuller went to a meeting of German church people who were trying to decide whether the church had any responsibility for the Nazi conflagration. After the first day's meeting they concluded they were quite innocent. They tried to fight off Hitler but failed. That night Pastor Niemuller had a dream. He suddenly found himself bathed in a beam of light. He knew it was the light of God's presence and was filled with awe. Then behind him he unmistakenly heard the voice of Hitler saying, "Martin, Martin, why didn't you ever tell me?" He awoke and did not sleep the rest of the night reflecting on his relationship with Hitler. He thought of the many ways he had failed to bring the claim of Jesus Christ upon Hitler and the people around him. Once, he actually spent two hours with Hitler. He never mentioned Jesus Christ or his Christian faith. The next day he went before the German church group and shared his reflections. They reversed their decision and took their share of the responsibility for what Hitler had done.

If we are not open to the possibility of God speaking like this, we can cut off the graceful actions of God toward us. I try to listen to other people and their dreams as if I am listening to God. Brooks said, "No one will ever open their soul to us until we view that person as a holy, divine creation in which the divine resides." Only as I have this attitude will people reveal the depths of themselves and their most personal dreams.

After a person tells me a dream, the first thing I do is try to learn about the outer circumstances around that dream. What crisis is the person facing? The dream may prod the person to tell of things he or she has never talked about before. If the discussion of the dream does not prompt this, I may ask, "What does the dream mean to you?" If the self-interpretation makes sense, I can show how it does—that is more helpful than my interpretation. Learning to interpret one's own dreams is the ultimate goal. Even when I am working with people who send accounts of dreams by mail, I ask that they try to give their own interpretation. Sometimes I suggest that they also try to give the message of the dream in a sentence or two. I may point out certain aspects, but my task is to encourage the dreamer to trust in his or her own perceptions.

If I still have little understanding of the dream, I ask for associations to the various dream symbols and figures. First I seek for the personal associations before looking for the archetypal meanings. One of my criticisms of many Jungians is that because they are so interested in archetypal themes they sometimes neglect dealing with the ordinary personal and historical data. Our first interest should naturally be in personal associations to dream figures. In my book *Dreams, A Way to Listen to God*, I indicate some of the meanings beyond the personal that can be given by dream symbols.

After the associations have been given, I offer suggestions as to what the meaning might be. *My suggestion is correct only when it makes sense to the other person.* If I am sure that I am correct and the person cannot accept what I suggest, it is better to go onto something else rather than insist on my meaning. If the person continues to work with dreams, the Lord of dreams will provide another dream with the message needed for the next phase of growth. My suggestions are nearly always tentative rather than definitive. I need to respect the pace of growth and development that is natural for the other person.

The counselor or spiritual director should begin a study of dream symbolism. There are different ways to go about this. Someone skilled in the meaning of dream symbols is most helpful. My fifteen years in Jungian analysis provided the best laboratory for getting at the meaning of symbols. I have continued to discuss my dreams with two therapist friends, John Sanford and Andrew Canale. Not everyone can have this opportunity, but this does not mean that one is cut short. One can find an intuitive friend to listen and also supplement the learning through reading. I recommend John Sanford's books *Dreams, God's Forgotten Language* and *Dreams and Healing.* One can look at the dream section in my *Adventure Inward* and at *Dreams, A Way to Listen to God,* as well as reading Jung's own works on the subject. One volume collects much of what Jung wrote on the subject. Its title is transparent: *Dreams.* The index to Jung's *Collected Works* is remarkably helpful in that it lists most dream symbols that are interpreted in his writings.

Many years ago I had an ecstatic dream experience. I dreamed that I made love to Rhea, the mother of the gods, and then, when I was alone afterward, I held in my hand a blue crystal of copper sulfate. Next in the dream I realized that the church should have three parts: a sanctuary for worship; rooms for discussion, small group meetings, education, growth, and prayer, and other rooms for individual counseling.

When I awoke I looked at several of Jung's books trying to find out about the symbolism of the copper sulfate. I found that copper represented the feminine, sulfur the masculine. The crystal was a symbol of wholeness within me. Out of this wholeness came a vision for the church, which we implemented at St. Luke's in Monrovia, California.

I would not have understood this vision without Jung's wealth of knowledge about symbolism. If Jung had spent his time trying to integrate his basic findings into the church, he might not have left such a vast legacy of knowledge. John Sanford is in a similar position. He is studying the dream for its own sake rather than continually relating it to the church. I see my task as taking the data of people and trying to integrate them into Christianity.

It is helpful to distinguish between a sign and a symbol. A sign is an image that has one clear meaning. A symbol is an image that represents a psychic reality with all the dozens of meanings within it. Psychic reality, like physical reality, is indefinable. Dreams talk most of the time in symbols, not in signs. So there are deeper levels of meaning in nearly all dreams. Somebody once asked me if all dreams are from God, if all are important. Yes, they are, but sometimes God gives us a dream just bursting with meaning. Some dreams are like garden dirt, others are like radium. We must work like a physicist to discover the significance hidden in the dirt.

When I am working with people on dreams I usually ask them to summarize the dream in writing and outline a plan of action suggested by the dream: either a method of avoiding a negative situation that is described, or actualizing the positive with some kind of definite action. This method of dream study will not hurt anyone and might open some of us to the voice of the loving God.

Synchronicity

It is difficult for many people to see the relevance of dreams because they are caught in a causally determined universe. A causes B causes C and so on, ad infinitum. This is a closed system in which one physical event is the total cause of another. This theory is the causal theory of the space-time box. Jung suggested another theory. He never denied causality, but he did not believe that it accounted for all events. He called these events that did not fit the causal system acausal, or synchronistic, events. He saw a meaning in each instant of time, a coherence in every period of duration. This was not due to physical causation, but to Spirit. The Chinese called this Tao. Jung wrote a detailed description of this phenomenon. Figure 6 may help explain his meaning.

In figure 6, A causes B, and this causes C. In synchronicity, each moment, A, B, C, D, etc., is related to all other events in that given moment and to the flow of meaning represented by the wavy band at the top.

Dream interpretation rests upon the principle that each moment of time is meaningful in terms of spiritual reality. A dream does not cause an

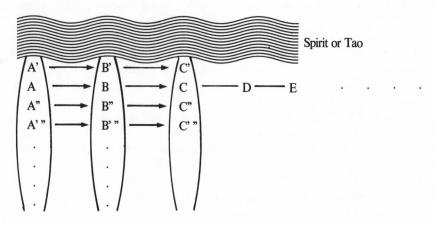

Figure 6

external event to happen when it gives telepathic or precognitive data. Rather, it synchronously expresses what is being manifested outside.

Synchronicity does not operate through dreams alone. Another common use of this principle among Christians is opening a Bible at random and putting the finger down on a verse to suggest God's meaning for us at that time. Oracles operate on the same principle. We need to be careful not to use this method as a replacement for our intelligence, but in conjunction with, and in addition to, our intelligence. Sometimes dreams and oracles can give us clues when we are caught in darkness with no sense of a way out.

When Saul came to the witch (medium) of Endor, he said that God did not speak to him any more in dreams, nor by the Urim, nor by the prophets, and he was lost (1 Sam. 28:6). What were the Urim and the Thummim? They were an Old Testament method of the sacred casting of lots. Even today Mennonite bishops are selected by the casting of lots: a group of candidates is chosen and a Bible for each candidate is placed on an altar. Each Bible has a slip of paper in it, one of which is longer than the others. Each candidate selects a Bible. The one who chooses the book with the longest slip of paper is the new bishop.

There is considerable historical precedence for listening to dreams and sacred oracles. If we are too preoccupied with listening for clues, we are silly. But if we use this method in cooperation with the intellect it helps us see Jung's idea that we live in a unified reality where nothing is meaningless. Each moment has its own deep reality. The use of the I Ching is based on this principle. That ancient oracular text is probably closer to the New Testament than any other sacred book from non-Christian traditions.

The technique I am referring to should be used only under the guidance of the Holy Spirit. This practice can be evil if used for our personal gain or to cause harm. Unless one has a background in theology and critical thinking, it is wise to stay away from such things so as not to be swept off one's feet. It is better for such a person to stick with traditional practices. However, if we are guiding others on the spiritual way we need to know about such widespread practices and not be afraid of them. C. S. Lewis once observed that God takes a lot of trouble to hide the meaning of the future. Rather than trying to figure out what will be, we should flow as wisely as we can with the meaning of the moment. Prayer, meditation, and active imagination can help us greatly in accomplishing this goal.

As for the I Ching, if we see the Tao as the Logos of the loving Christ, we transpose it into a Christian frame of reference. Jung's concept of synchronicity gives the framework for taking seriously dreams, active imagination, ESP, and the casting of sacred lots. As I move into harmony with the divine will, I make changes that result in a new series of events. Thus, through prayer, active imagination, and the heeding of dreams I can be an instrument for a flow of inner and outer events more in accord with God's Kingdom and will. Therefore my Christian prayer may make me more effective as a person in this world.

Jung told a story about Brother Klaus, a Swiss monk who lived not far from Zurich. Brother Klaus was a devout person of great spirituality and holiness. He was venerated throughout his country. The Swiss were trying to arrive at confederation, but they were unsuccessful. A bloody civil war seemed imminent. When Brother Klaus learned of this danger he came to the meeting place in Zurich where the deliberations were taking place. He sat down in back of the hall and said nothing. His presence was felt and the deliberations continued, compromises were made on both sides, and resolution was achieved. The modern Swiss federation dates to this time. Holiness can have practical consequences.

Chapter 12

ARCHETYPES OR
SPIRITUAL ENTITIES?

The natural universe, in the Jungian sense of the term natural, contains physical and spiritual dimensions. A person who acknowledges only the reality of the physical realm is incapable of recognizing how synchronicity operates in the New Testament and in our world and cannot see the power of the spiritual. By contrast, a person who goes to the other extreme, who sees reality only in the spiritual realm and denies reality in the physical world, will not spend much time bettering the world and will fall readily into superstition. I find the *Tibetan Book of the Dead* an example of the latter problem. Although we can learn much from it, it lacks consistency and never comes down to reality. Being totally involved in the psychic dimension, without connection with the earth, can lead to psychosis.

Zen Buddhism methodically transports a person out of the physical realm and into the spiritual. One can get lost in the world of images, the world of the devil, Makyo, and succumb to what is known as "Zen madness"— getting lost in the psychoid world. To avoid such a fate each of us who is interested in spiritual reality should be certain that we are in significant caring relatedness with other people. Some courses in the basic sciences, like chemistry and physics, can help keep us grounded. Ironically though, chemistry and physics at their most advanced level, actually integrate the insights of synchronicity more than most theology or Bible courses.

In order to understand archetypes we need to be very specific. A recent dream of mine can help us in our understanding: I was in the kitchen mixing a concoction of many different kinds of liquor. The unconscious is not above punning: we speak of alcohol as "spirits." In the dream, I mixed quarts of scotch, gin, and vodka. Then I added an ingredient to give the mixture solidity. It tasted like rum balls, but infinitely more delicious. I wanted to share my discovery with others. Then I was at a fancy party with my son, John, who in actuality is very close to the unconscious. I was in the kitchen preparing the hors d'oeuvres with what was brought by me and others. In a sense, this dream depicts the role of the ego as that of blending the different ingredients presented from the spiritual and social realms to come up with nourishment and enjoyment for oneself and others. The archetype of the alchemist or priest-shaman underlies the dream.

Second only to the archetype of the self (the Holy Spirit in Christian terminology), that of the ego is of paramount importance. Some people know nothing but the ego and identify with it exclusively. Then the ego becomes a persona, which is the Greek word for mask. When we meet an ego-identified person we are meeting only a mask, not a real person. When the mask is dropped, the person often goes through an ego-death experience, which can be very frightening; it can cause disaster or it can spur the person on to new life. At one point in my spiritual journey, in order to hide my ministerial persona, I wore argyle socks with my black suit and turned collar to show that I was no longer identified with that role—but I really showed only how caught up in it I still was. Giving up the persona is inevitably painful. It takes time to adapt to a new orientation. We are putting off an old skin so we can grow a new one.

In thirty years of working on my dreams I discovered many aspects of me, including many archetypal factors. I have referred already to these earlier, but now is the time to explore them further. The first archetype I found within me was that of the inner mother and inner child. I did not have much of a relationship with my father, but I was very close to my mother, which created a mother complex. According to most Freudian thought, this complex is psychopathological. Jung writes that the mother complex can be the source of great gifts: a sensitivity to others, an artistic ability, a capacity to teach, an understanding of history, and an openness to the spiritual dimension. It is destructive only when it possesses us. I was certainly helped very much when Hilde Kirsch demanded, "Morton, when are you going to stop thinking that your parents' attitude toward you is gospel?"

As a small child I was sickly, slightly spastic, and could not speak plainly. My parents thought that I was retarded. Whatever validity their other perceptions had, that one was wrong. In the third grade, when I took the Stanford-Binet intelligence test, my parents realized that dimwittedness was not my problem. In coming into my own, I had to disidentify with that early picture of myself. That was one essential meaning of my dream about making love with Rhea, the mother of the gods. It was a symbolic bringing into conjunction of the masculine and feminine, after which the mother complex would no longer dominate me as it had. For a man, the well-integrated feminine can be a source of creativity almost beyond measure. The trick is staying in touch with this complex without being possessed by it.

I had many dreams of the idiot child. I had to learn to kiss it and so allow it to become the divine child who already knows the spiritual world. When I am possessed by the frightened little idiot who has been mistreated by life, I can panic and run from my responsibilities. When I embrace that inner child, it is the idiot no longer, and can bring me a sense of openness and wonder, playfulness and joy. In *The Elephant Man*, when the sophisticated and intelligent doctor embraces John Merrick, the freak becomes a beautiful, creative soul. No wonder this film touched so many of us who, on a deep level, view ourselves as freaks rather than human beings. There is usually a connection between the archetype of the mother and that of the child. When one has been overshadowed by the mother, it causes damage to the child within. Hence, both archetypes need realignment.

Venus (or Aphrodite) is one of the best-known archetypal figures in our male-dominated society. Each person has a symbol that carries this archetype: Marilyn Monroe fulfilled this role for many. Venus was *the* significant archetype in Freud's system. He interpreted the whole psyche in terms of it. Jung knew that Venus could be an enormous source of power, personality, energy, and libido, but he believed she was only one aspect of the source. This figure can lead us totally astray or she can be the divine inspirer. In moments of realization, when we are awed by the beauty of our beloved, we can penetrate into the presence of the divine mystery. This can bring heaven to earth, as Charles Williams explains in his study of Dante, *The Figure of Beatrice*.

Father Jupiter (or Zeus) with his lightning bolts and power is another archetypal figure. When he possesses me, I can be the slave trader, the businessman who with no compassion grinds opponents under his heel, the paterfamilias who dominates wife and children and anyone else who comes his way. This is Adler's basic archetype. We can gain many insights about it from studying Adler, but should be wary of Adler's tendency to interpret the whole psyche in terms of it. Adler can teach us much about power and Jehovah, just as we can learn much valuable about Venus and sex from Freud. Jung's system leaves room in which to integrate both Freud and Adler, and many other aspects of ourselves, as well.

In my pantheon of archetypes, Mercury, the divine youth, is a central one. For a woman, this figure can be the sex symbol. When an older woman gets caught by this archetype she can destroy both young men and herself. For a man, the youth can lend freshness, hope, and vitality, along with a questing, innovative, questioning spirit. But if a man is dominated by it, he can remain unsettled, rebellious, and unfulfilled in career or marriage. Mercury (or Hermes) was also the intermediary between the gods and human beings and so became the archetype of the priest-shaman for me.

No archetypal power is more fearful than Mars (or Ares). He can be the collective murderer or the savior of civilization, depending on whether he is aggressive or defensive. Each one of us has this warrior within, this power which can either murder or support all that is good and holy.

I remember clearly my first realization that such a power was within me. I used to think of myself as a gentle, kindly fellow. Then I had the following dream: I was sitting on the porch of my childhood home looking over some empty lots between our house and the church we attended, the same one near which I first learned the unspeakableness of sexuality. A bomb exploded in a vacant lot between the two buildings. A mushroom cloud emerged out of the explosion. From that cloud emerged a warrior in black armor charging on a black horse with lance set. Upon waking I wondered how that figure could relate to me. Although I had painted this figure, I resisted the message of the dream because it went against so many layers of my persona.

Then I had another dream. I was talking to a forest ranger in a woods where I had leased a cabin. Red the Ranger was his name. In waking life I treated such an official with great respect and care. However, in this dream I told him what I thought of him, his ancestry, his descendants, and his dog. I told this dream to my analyst, who said, "Of course you realize the forest ranger is a part of you—the unrelenting, stupid, resistant, illogical, bureaucratic, dominating part of you." I said, "I am not like that." We let it go at that. When I returned home, my wife asked, "How did it go?" I answered, "I wasted my money." She asked, "Why did you waste your money?" "Hilde didn't understand me and gave me a totally erroneous dream interpretation," I complained. So I told her the dream. "You certainly did waste your money," Barbara concurred, "I could have told you the same thing." My psychological resistance was so great that I did not believe my wife, either. When the children came home from school, one by one I asked for their interpretations. They all agreed with their mother. One of the most important realizations of my life was that I had a side of me like that. I really had not known that I could come across with such anger, rigidity, and power. But my wife and children lived with this fellow.

It is important to recognize our archetypes; otherwise, we have no way of preventing them from making us into what they are, no way to keep them from possessing us. When we are possessed we express a limited part of the whole, and fall into evil. (Evil is any secondary good which pretends to be the best.) Jesus expressed the whole. He showed the same kind of strength and power in his opposition to the Pharisees. He could even walk to his own crucifixion carrying the cross. That is wholeness. Jesus is not an archetype. He is the harmony of all of them working together for the glory and the coming of the Kingdom.

I am not strong enough to handle the powerful spiritual forces within me. They are more powerful than I. I need divine aid so that they will not dominate me. I know of no way other than a religious one to handle archetypes. Without that inner warrior though, I become a spineless, weak, sentimental person with no ability to stand up for my convictions. Thanks to that warrior within, I have been able to persist like a lonely voice crying in the wilderness to express my views on the Christian message of love. As others recognized the validity of what I was saying, my warrior stand was confirmed. Likewise, Venus has given me the capacity to love, and the child brings me humility and wonder.

The priest-shaman, being a channel for the divine, is presently my dominant archetype. We might doubt that this one could ever be destructive, but it surely can. The value of a shaman depends upon the deity he or she mediates. In a series of papers now collected in *Civilization in Transition,* Jung states that the basic problem of Nazi Germany was the worship of Wotan rather than Christ. In this perspective, Hitler was a shaman, but for a dangerous and fickle deity. The priests of Mexico were mediators for an Aztec deity. The Aztecs went to war for the primary purpose of bringing back sacrificial victims. Tens of thousands of young men were sacrificed every year. Now and then some pathological person will be gripped by this archetype, and lure young men into his power to murder them. The archetype of the Aztec priest still lives under its dominance. Instead of sacrificing ourselves, we sacrifice others. How easily archetypes can turn demonic.

The archetypal professor appears to be an innocent person, provided that he is in touch with the spiritual world and the Christ and that he submits his intelligence to the divine. But the professor in me got me so wound up in Immanuel Kant and rationalist philosophy that he led me into an anxiety neurosis. He convinced me there was no logical reason for a spiritual world that could break through to me. Once converted, the same professor wrote twenty books. He is still going strong. In himself, he is neither good nor bad. His value depends upon the one to whom he owes allegiance. It is good to remember that C. S. Lewis's horror story *That Hideous Strength* was set in an English university town.

My last two archetypes are the least well developed in me. One is the merrymaker, the fool. The other is Vulcan, known to the Greeks as He-phaestus, the smith at the forge who deals with hard, cold reality. He is a marvelous counterbalance for the professor. He likes to make things with his hands. He also likes to dig in the dirt and plant gardens. When he is not taken seriously because we are becoming too ethereal, he often strikes the body with physical illness. When I neglect the earthy side of me, when I fail to run and exercise, to work in the dirt and fix leaky roofs, I ignore my own body, which God made and which is good. My fool can lighten the load of all my more serious archetypes with his sense of humor and playfulness. But negatively, he can too readily push the panic button if he dominates, as he does not have the practical skills for coping with reality and its stresses.

The question often arises as to whether these archetypes are personal or transpersonal. They are both. I need to know them well, because the moment I lose my persona and realize that I cannot manage my life by my will alone, I find many inner powers and personalities that would rush in to fill the breach and rule. If I let any one of them do so, I can be destroyed. There is a principle of darkness that seeks to undermine my soul by tempting me to identify with one of the archetypes. Jesus Christ, the son of the living God, the Creator of heaven and earth, says, "Come and be in fellowship with me, and I will help you bring all of these forces into harmony and defeat the works of evil." Only in and through a savior can I bring harmony to my soul. It does not matter whether we call Christ by his name. Whatever the name, the same reality brings us to unity. In my opinion, the Christ is the most concrete and easily followed represen-tation of this principle. Jung confirms in a different terminology the Christian atonement experience: I need to give up my own selfish will as the ultimate solution to my life's problems and enter into a cooperative venture with this healing reality if I am ever to find harmony and creativ-ity.

Whenever I react with inappropriate emotion to my situation, an archetype or complex is usually operating. One way I can monitor the archetypes is by observing my emotions, my moods, and my antipathies. Other ways are by dreams, the imagination, and by what literature at-tracts me. *Playboy* magazine is as dedicated to Venus as any temple on the Mediterranean shore.

It is crucial for us to be able to discern and distinguish the positive from the negative in the realm of archetypes. How can we do this? The New Testament speaks of angels and demons. These are powers and mes-sengers of creation and destruction. The archetypes are angels in the hands of Christ and devils in the hands of the Evil One. Every human being needs salvation, which means divine help. Salvation does not come cheap, or else God would not have gone to the trouble of securing it for us with Christ's death on the cross.

Anybody under the illusion of being strong enough to play with the demonic may come to tragedy. The figure of Satan and a destructive element trying to bind us to fragmentedness is not a children's story. We live in a physical world much more complex and mysterious than we think; the psychic one is stranger still. Yet to be overawed by the demonic aspect of the psychic is to forget that Christ has given us power over it. It has no ultimate power over us when we are in Christ's presence. The film *The Exorcist* presents very bad theology. It lacks the understanding that Christ died on the cross so that the exorcist does not have to die in exorcising. On the whole, the best kind of exorcism is truly loving a person so that the Evil One is gradually pushed out.

We human beings are much deeper than we think. Some people who do not know human psychology treat as demonic possession what is really a weak ego structure in which the archetypal powers may take over at any time. The way to heal this condition is to strengthen the personality structure so that the person can resist these powers and turn to God. Exorcising someone with a weak ego is dangerous for many reasons: it is futile, it keeps the person from the kind of treatment that can help, and it can lead to despair. Perhaps exorcism may occasionally be useful, but only after consultation with two or three people who know depth psychology, and only when there is a willingness to follow up with loving care. Exorcism implies that the Evil One has possessed a person at some point. Most of what is today called possession is psychosomatic illness, anxiety neurosis with hyperventilation and hysterical and compulsive symptoms, or borderline psychosis.

There are several concrete ways to distinguish the divine from the demonic.[1] First, it is possible to observe whether the action of power comes from a coherent and respected religious tradition. Anyone who claims to have a new religion may well have an inflated ego and is probably in the hands of the Evil One. Jesus made only two or three minor changes in Judaism. The reason he came among the Jews was that the Old Testament offered the best religion that God had been able to create up to that time, and Jesus could make as few changes as possible. The second way to distinguish between the divine and the demonic is to judge whether the action, personality, or power in question results in love and harmony or in hate and schism. The Lord of the Flies, as Satan is called in some New Testament passages, loves to infiltrate the church and cause hate and schism. The third criterion can be seen in the example of Jesus, who spoke with authority but not with finality. Anyone who proposes totally final, never changeable definitive answers is probably operating under the influence of evil rather than under that of Jesus Christ and is probably bent on brainwashing people.

A fourth standard of discernment is to see whether the fruits of an action or way of life reveal its angelic inspiration and guidance. Does an act lead to creativity, growth, development, increased consciousness, keener awareness, and the other gifts of the spirit described by Saint Paul as "Love, joy, peace, patient endurance, kindness, generosity, faith, mildness, justice" (Gal. 5:22–23)? Demonic influence results in disintegration, narrowed awareness, stunted growth, hate, and schism. One nearly sure sign of demonic power is the attempt on the part of one person or group to gain power over others and seek from them an attitude of subservience. The angelic, however, stimulates freedom and open, honest exchange between people. The demonic favors bondage, subservience, and class distinction. The angelic seeks to promote an atmosphere of encounter, love, and interchange. The demonic fosters dependency.

Slavery is one of the worst human evils in that it justifies using another person as an object. Prostitution is a kind of slavery: the sexual act is not as immoral as the fact that one person owns another for a period of time. When a person gets inflated and feels perfect and projects the shadow and darkness onto others, that is a certain sign of demonic influence. A critical, negative, judgmental attitude toward others results from an inflated opinion of our own self. The angelic seldom speaks of its own perfection. Historically, the saints were constantly speaking of themselves as the worst of sinners.

Last of all, a sure mark of the demonic is a destructive depression, a voice that says within, "you are no good, you never will be any good, your life is worthless." That is nearly always the voice of the Evil One. Christ died to relieve us from that kind of destructive inner voice. The savior has conquered evil and has dominion over the demonic and the archetypes.

NOTES

1. See my book *Discernment* for an expanded discusson of this topic, pp. 79ff.

Chapter 13

RELATING TO THE UNCONSCIOUS: ACTIVE IMAGINATION AND MEDITATION

Our next task is to examine how we can enter into a creative dialogue with our unconscious through the use of active imagination and meditation. Before treating this topic directly, it will be helpful to clarify the meaning of the words we will use.

An archetype has quite a different meaning from a complex. The former is basically a collective and partially transpersonal phenomenon; the latter is more personal. My friend Max Zeller was imprisoned by the Nazis in a concentration camp. Through a series of remarkable events he was released and his life was saved. But he told me that whenever he heard marching feet, his tension level rose and his heart began palpitating as he recalled those Nazi feet marching down the hallway to his apartment to take him away. This is a perfect example of a complex.

Another example of a complex is found in the preceding chapter. When I wrote about the Father Zeus archetype, I mentioned none of its positive attributes. As I reviewed the chapter I was struck by this omission, which is truly a Freudian slip. My own personal relationship with my father kept me from mentioning the positive aspects of this archetype. On the positive side, the father archetype is the ruler, the one who brings order, structure, discipline, and responsibility. I am much indebted to my father for giving me some of these qualities.

A further distinction needs to be made between the specific male and female archetypes on the one hand, and the animus and anima on the other. A woman's animus is the sum of her various masculine archetypes which together constitute the masculine aspects of her personality. Likewise, the anima encompasses the feminine archetypes in a man, in my case Venus and the great mother Ceres (or Demeter). Consequently the terms animus and anima are more inclusive than the separate archetypes.

While on this subject, I need to state quite frankly that I know far less about the feminine psyche than the masculine. The best I can do to compensate for this is to recommend some further reading. Adolf Guggenbühl-Craig's books are excellent: *Marriage—Dead or Alive* and *Power in the Helping Profession*. Although slightly dated, Esther Harding's books *The Way of All Women* and *Women's Mysteries* are excellent; both draw heavily on mythological lore to depict the feminine psyche and the second is one of the best treatments of the subject that I know. *Knowing Woman*, by Irene de Castillejo, emphasizes the fact that women have a more diffused awareness than men, who tend to be more focused. The animus helps a woman to focus her consciousness. Erich Neumann's *The Great Mother* is another classic study of the feminine.

When we begin the inner journey we pass beyond our conscious personality and are likely to confront our shadow, all those rejected contents of the psyche. Much of the pain of an anxiety neurosis is caused by being confronted by our shadow. As already mentioned, the shadow is usually 90 percent pure gold. It needs to be released from repression and confronted. It contains the positive and negative powers of the archetypes and complexes as well as our personal unconscious. Beyond the shadow we encounter the anima and animus, our contrasexual sides. These present persistent problems as long as we live; we need to continue adapting to the animus and the anima, as they demand an ongoing relationship.

Dialogue with the unconscious and its contents is often necessary as we work toward wholeness and integration. In most dreams, the different personal figures usually represent parts of myself. Yet, in the dream of Michael appearing to his mother after his death, we have an objective psychic reality. A dream with that kind of numinous power often reveals the transpersonal. We need to be constantly aware of the different levels involved in the unconscious.

Archetypal dreams emerge in young children. Children's dreams should not be interpreted, for this calls too much attention to them and focuses them too much on the unconscious. Children may be encouraged to draw their dreams if they are bothered by them, talk about them, or tell stories about them, but adults should not interpret them. Frances Wickes' *The Inner World of Childhood* is a magnificent study of children. It helped me to unscramble my unhappy childhood more than any other book I have read. The author was a Jungian analyst who worked with children in New York. She wrote the final revision of the book when she was over the age of ninety. She saw as clients the grandchildren of her first patients. Her wisdom is deep. The book is a marvelous way to start reading and understanding Jung's view on childhood.

If life events lead to a shattering of the persona and the contents of the unconscious stream into awareness without time for a slow orderly dialogue, an emergency arises. The person feels as if death is imminent. In such a crisis, the only thing that can protect us is to find someone who can help us do group therapy with our rampaging archetypes and who can help us seek the divine lover within. Often, people who are not given such help come to the brink of suicide. The church has a critically important ministry in this area.

Many people lead fairly satisfactory lives until the age of thirty-five or forty, when they suddenly fall apart as they face the meaninglessness of their lives. Alcohol dulls us to the pain, but solves nothing. The ensuing sickness of being caught in an existential vacuum can be just as severe as that caused by childhood beatings, neglect, and sexual abuse. Only counselors or clergy who recognize the nature of the existential crisis can help the sufferer. Sometimes only a person with a spiritual perspective is able to help, since most secular psychologists are not comfortable in this area. In such a crisis we need someone who can guide the dialogue with the unconscious all the way through to a living source of faith.

What I call archetypes were known to traditional Christianity by other names: the cardinal sins and virtues, the angels and demons, the pagan gods. Comic-strip characters are also usually archetypal in nature. Many of Jung's books deal with archetypes, but in particular *The Archetypes and the Collective Unconscious.*

The unconscious and the spiritual realm can be approached in two quite different ways. The first is the way of imagelessness, which scholars call the apophatic approach. It is described by Evagrius and Dionysius the Areopagite. In some of their writings, Saint Teresa and Saint John of the Cross follow this tradition, as does Thomas Merton in our own century. This point of view is exaggerated and debased in Adolf Tanquerey's *The Spiritual Life.* That book ruined spirituality for many seekers in the Catholic Church, for the spiritual is set over against the human.

The second approach is the method of Saint Augustine, of most of the church fathers, and of the medieval church. It was formalized in the spiritual exercises of Ignatius of Loyola. Loyola systematized what was a common practice in nearly every medieval monastery and convent. Loyola's method is still viable, when combined with psychological insight. We must, however, overlook his attitude toward women, which is closer to that of Buddha than to that of Jesus Christ.

Jung's method is very similar to the imaginative tradition that had been central to monastic life in Europe for centuries. Active imagination, according to Jung, is the process of opening oneself to the depth of the psyche and letting the images flow while at the same time keeping a personal standpoint. By this method one can reach to the spiritual world and the divine. Jung developed this practice as he was passing through his own dark night. It is difficult to describe the process. Active imagination, like meditation, is best learned in the laboratory of experience with the help of one who has gone this way already. In my book *Adventure Inward* I show many examples of this process.

Jung developed active imagination to deal with his own integration and then he discovered that it helped his patients as well. He gave the following example of this practice:

> I was treating a young artist, and he had the greatest trouble in understanding what I meant by active imagination. He tried all sorts of things but he could not get at it. The difficulty with him was that he could not think. Musicians, painters, artists of all kinds, often can't think at all, because they never intentionally use their brain. This man's brain too was always working for itself; it had its artistic imaginations and he couldn't use it psychologically, so he couldn't understand. I gave him every chance to try, and he tried all sorts of stunts. I cannot tell you all the things he did, but I will tell you how he finally succeeded in using his imagination psychologically.
>
> I live outside the town, and he had to take the train to get to my place. It starts from a small station, and on the wall of that station was a poster. Each time he waited for his train he looked at that poster. The poster was an advertisement for Mürren in the Bernese Alps, a colorful picture of waterfalls, of a green meadow and a hill in the center, and on that hill were several cows. So he sat there staring at that poster and thinking that he could not find out what I meant by active imagination. And then one day he thought: "Perhaps I could start by having a fantasy about that poster. I might for instance imagine that I am myself in the poster, that the scenery is real and that I could walk up the hill among the cows and then look down on the other side, and then I might see what is behind that hill."[1]

I have used this passage many times in working with groups on journal keeping and meditation. I suggest that they get quiet and try to get into the scene that I read to them. I ask them to imagine what they see on the other side of the hill. Of course, each person sees what is in his or her own psyche. It is like a Rorschach test. Yet, there are usually collective patterns that emerge: some people see an abyss or a steep cliff; others see a hill, a town, or often a river. I then read what Jung's patient imagined:

> So he went to the station for that purpose and imagined that he was in the poster. He saw the meadow and the road and walked up the hill

among the cows, and then he came up to the top and looked down, and there was the meadow again, sloping down, and below was a hedge with a stile. So he walked down and over the stile, and there was a little footpath that ran round a ravine, and a rock, and when he came round that rock, there was a small chapel, with its door standing a little ajar. He thought he would like to enter, and so he pushed the door open and went in, and there upon an altar decorated with pretty flowers stood a wooden figure of the Mother of God. He looked up at her face, and in that exact moment something with pointed ears disappeared beind the altar. He thought, "Well, that's all nonsense," and instantly the whole fantasy was gone.

He went away and said, "Now again I haven't understood what active imagination is." And then, suddenly, the thought struck him: "Well, perhaps that really *was* there: perhaps that thing behind the Mother of God, with the pointed ears, that disappeared like a flash, really happened." Therefore he said to himself: "I will just try it all over as a test." So he imagined that he was back in the station looking at the poster, and again he fantasied that he was walking up the hill. And when he came to the top of the hill, he wondered what he would see on the other side. And there was the hedge and the stile and the hill sloping down. He said, "Well, so far so good. Things haven't moved since, apparently." And he went round the rock, and there was the chapel. He said: "There is the chapel, that at least is no illusion. It is all quite in order." The door stood ajar and he was quite pleased. He hesitated a moment and said: "Now, when I push that door open and I see the Madonna on the altar, then that thing with the pointed ears should jump down behind the Madonna, and if it doesn't, then the whole thing is bunk!" And so he pushed the door open and looked— and there it all was and the thing jumped down, as before, and then he was convinced. From then on he had the key and knew he could rely on his imagination, and so he learned to use it.

This is a secular use of precisely the same kind of process that Saint Ignatius uses in the spiritual exercises. When one makes such encounters with the unconscious it is wise to keep a record of them. Writing down these fantasies helps to keep us grounded in reality. Working with the imagination without a journal is like being a chemist without test tubes or beakers.

In order to open ourselves to spontaneous imagination, we need first to quiet down in body and mind. Without that preliminary, we continue in ego patterns and daydreams rather than unconscious fantasy. Daydreams are consciously directed. But in active imagination we open a door and see things we never expected to see. We are constantly surprised. Silence is necessary to this state of mind. Breathing deeply and quietly is another prerequisite. Choosing a quiet place helps us come to this frame of mind. All other concerns need to be put aside. We can focus on an object or a repeated syllable, or try to be totally removed from all sensation. The middle of the night is the time I find most conducive to this state. When we get up in the middle of the night for active imagination, we are already quiet and do not have to spend time quieting down.

When I was working with Max Zeller, I arrived at his office one day and he said, "You look awful. What's bothering you?" "I can't sleep at night," I answered. "I go to bed at nine, ten, or eleven; sleep four or five hours, and wake up. I feel totally awake and can't go back to sleep. I have a fourteen-hour day ahead of me and don't know how I am going to get through it." Max said, "Do you know why you can't sleep at night?" I expected a psychologically sophisticated answer from him. I said, "No, why?" He said, "God wants to talk with you. That's the way he got in touch with Samuel, didn't He? Do you think He's changed?"

If we are suffering, we may even be crazy enough to get up in the middle of the night. Some thirty years ago I took up my journal at two o'clock in the morning and went to the only warm room in the house and sat down and wrote:

Me: Well, Lord, here I am. A friend told me to come here in the middle of the night and ask You what You had on Your mind. Are You there? Do You wish to talk to me? You know I need and want my sleep.
[Whenever one talks to the Lord, one should be honest.]
Voice: I want you, my child, and I want to help you because of what you are capable of becoming. I love you and I want to give you that love.
Me: Well, why don't You do it at a reasonable time?
Voice: I can never get your attention. You're so busy that if I'm to break through with love and concern for you, I must make you uncomfortable and wake you up in the middle of the night when you wouldn't think of doing anything else.
Me: If it hadn't been for Max Zeller, I might never have understood the message. I might have gone down the drain. That hardly seems like kindness and concern.
Voice: Just because you have forgotten how to listen to the depth is no reason that I am not who I am. It is not My fault that you have not heard the message of Scripture in church. I'm always here and seeking your fellowship. You've been so caught up with the outer world.
Me: Why do You want me? I am of no value; You must know all my faults and lusts and angers. How could You love me?
Voice: Child, child, how little you understand. I am love. I can no more help loving you human beings than a leopard can change its spots. It is My nature to love, and I have created all human beings because I love them and want them to respond to Me. I long for them to stop and receive My love.
Me: You mean You care for me, with all my stupidity, anger, self-will, and egotism?
Voice: This is the whole point of My being. I would have died for you if you had been the only human being. It is your very need for Me that makes My love flow even more. Those who are getting along well in the world don't need My love as much as those who are lost, struggling and in pain.

Me: If You really care for me and if You are really there, I don't have to do it all on my own. I don't have to be afraid.

Voice: That's right, but before the day is over, you will forget this conversation, this encounter, and chalk it up to illusion. You will get busy and forget.

Me: What then would You have me do?

Voice: Have the courage to come back each night and get restored. Have the discipline to get up and talk with Me, even if you lose your sleep. Then during the day, pause and remember that I am with you and will help you through the day. Seek Me before you make any decisions or take any important actions. Remember I am here, that since I have conquered even death, you don't even have that to fear.

Me: I'll try to come back. Help me, Lord.

Then I went back to bed and to sleep.

This has been my practice for over thirty years. Out of these times of interaction with the divine lover have come most of my understanding of Scripture, most of my forgiving actions, my wisest and most charitable impulses, and most of the ideas for my books. It is a pure gift. Most people can have this kind of conversation. I record these meetings in my journal. Here is a passage from just a few days ago:

> I awake from a good night's sleep; dreams are just beyond the edge of recall. In my mind as I awake is the thought that I'll change my schedule or my life any way that You wish. I don't have to be set in cement. Then comes the realization that I live on the edge of an abyss and that when I am busy I fall into this abyss. I speak; what do you want, Lord?
>
> *Keep reflecting, and don't push yourself too hard. Also, don't feel afraid of a little tiredness. You may not need as much sleep as you thought. You drove yourself too hard yesterday.*
>
> What do I do?
>
> *Experiment with various plans, don't get caught up in one. I am with you. You don't have to finish this book by January 4 or 5. Life is really going well for you. Stay close to Me and My love. You are in a beautiful spot with one who truly loves you. I am here also. What more do you want?*
>
> I want to feel happy and contented all the time. Help me not to go into a snit when life is not exactly what I want it to be. I dread the next two lecturing trips.
>
> *Let go and flow with the current of My life and love. Have fun this day and see what the day brings.*
>
> I'll try.

One of the shortcomings of Ira Progoff's intensive journal method is that since he does not provide any belief in God as a divine lover, he does not see any desirability of this kind of daily contact with the unconscious depth.

Many years ago I dreamed that a big beautiful turtle came out of the

ocean and up onto the beach. The turtle was talking to me and its messages were very profound. However, when I woke up I could not remember what the turtle had said. I tried to reenter the dream as the young
artist had reentered the poster fantasy. I was back on the beach and imagined the turtle swimming toward me. It came up out of the water, but it
would not talk to me. Instead, it went over to a cliff behind me, knocked
three times on the cliff, and a door in the rock opened. I walked through
the door and entered a realm that I was to live in for four or five hours
each month for the next two years, until I had recorded some eighty
thousand words of fantasy. I could hardly believe what experiences spun
out of me. Many of the major myths of mankind spontaneously unfolded
around me. I learned that certain situations were perilous. I had to be
careful of them or I could get into psychic trouble. This experience was
an education in itself.

While dealing with the inner world in this way, I was careful not to
lose sight of the outer one. One of my annoyances with some Jungians is
that they get so caught up in the inner dimension that they often neglect
to make a good foundation in the outer one. Autobiography is useful to
that latter end. Our journal is a perfect place for that. One can autobio-
graphically seek to answer the following questions. Where did I come
from? How did I get here? Where am I? This helps me to know what
needs to be changed, and how I need to be transformed. There are several ways of going about this. One is to sit down and start writing an
autobiography. There is a simpler way, which I learned from Ira Progoff.
He suggests in his book *At a Journal Workshop* that we review our lives
and list eight to twelve events that were milestones in our lives. Limiting
the events to twelve spares us from the large task of writing a whole
autobiography and also gives a sense of structure.

My milestones were recalled as soon as I began to be quiet. The first
was birth and childhood sickness. The second was a sense of rejection,
weakness, and sickness as I grew older. The discovery of the body and of
sexuality came third. Fourth was the awareness of my intelligence, in
high school and in college. Fifth was the sickness and death of my mother
and the emotional struggles of living in an alien world. Sixth was the
beginning of some success in graduate school, physical discipline, and
parish work. Seventh was marriage, relationships, and children. Eighth
was coming to a dead-end street. Anxiety, analysis, and struggle were the
ninth milestone. Tenth was the discovery of the spiritual world and the
real significance of the Christian faith. That was ten years after I was
ordained a priest. The eleventh was a period of integrating spirit, mind,
and body. The twelfth I called doors opening, possibilities unfolding. This
outline gave me a ground to stand on and a perspective through which to

look at myself. Often classical Jungians underemphasize this kind of personal reflection.

My next exercise in spiritual autobiography was to list every major spiritual experience I could remember. The first was praying for my mother when she was sick and I was fourteen years old. She passed the crisis of her pneumonia and started toward recovery at the time I was praying. The rest of my list is recorded in *Adventures Inward.*

Another use of the active imagination is to hold a dialogue with an event or dream image from our past. A friend who is a middle-aged chemical engineer decided to have a dialogue with his wedding. This may sound childish, but Jesus taught us that as we become as little children, we enter the Kingdom of Heaven. For any creative use of the imagination, we need to be as little children. Here is the dialogue.

Me: Well, wedding, I'm not quite sure what it is you and I have to say to one another. You certainly were the offical kicking off point for something very significant in my life. And you have many brothers and sisters impacting the lives of others.

Wedding: Yes, that was a special day—my day! You and Dorothy brought a nice crowd to *my* wedding that day.

Me: I agree, there were all our good friends and our families and acquaintances. I'm glad you enjoyed them.

Wedding: June 29, 1962, 11:00 A.M. Yes, you were just barely there, I recall; but your wife really had it all planned and put together. All you had to do was show up and look appropriately happy.

Me: I may have looked that way, but oh boy I sure didn't feel that way. I was scared stiff and was asking myself every step if I really wanted to be part of your big show.

Wedding: And what did you decide?

Me: There was no choice at the time. There could be no change!

Wedding: If you had it to do over today, what would it be like?

Me: Well, I'd spend a lot more time knowing myself and I'd have a lot harder time deciding to "go ahead with it."

Wedding: And would you still have a wedding?

Me: I doubt if I would live alone, but I might choose to have women friends without all the entangling alliances.

Wedding: You like that freedom and independence?

Me: Yes, I suppose I would—at least for awhile.

Wedding: Well, that's way out of my field. My area is getting folks together, not pushing them apart. Well, so long.

Me: But I—wait, don't you offer any alternative?

Wedding: Nope, I'm a wedding—either you have me or you don't, so—see you around.

Me: (*sighing*) So long. I sure wish I knew if I really want you around or not!

This dialogue with an event of his life revealed to this man what he never consciously looked at before. He entered that wedding almost feeling manipulated, as though he had little or no choice. Until he could face that, he was unable to make a rapprochement with his wife. We cannot deal with what we do not know.

The active imagination can be helpful in resolving one's relationships with the deceased. My mother died when I was only twenty-one and I realized later that there was unfinished business between us. As the daughter and granddaughter of Presbyterian ministers, she was deeply stamped with the puritanism and Victorianism of the late nineteenth century. She was very loving and kind and had a tremendously positive influence on me. However, there were some negative influences and I realized I needed to talk with her. I imagined her in her prime. We were both adults. I pictured us walking along the brook by the church. I relived a scene from my early childhood. The following dialogue ensued:

Me:　Mother, I know you mean well, but you have certainly burdened me with rejection, dependence, devaluation of the body and sexuality, and given me a horrible sense of sin. I love you nonetheless, even though at times I am very angry at you and the evil which used you. But you also gave me the only love I had in childhood.

Mother:　As I told you not long before I died, it would have served me right if you had totally rejected me and ignored me.

Me:　That I could never do. I am not in any position to reject anyone. First you rejected me and turned me over to the maids; and then when you were alone with no one else caring for you, you overloved me, adding one sin to another. But there seems to be no way to raise children properly . . . I have lived out much of your repressed life. Can I be freed from it?

Mother:　There is more to our relationship than you say in your anger, but be as angry as you wish. You will not make me sick or upset me now. It is good for both of us to be honest. This will help to free both of us.

Me:　Why haven't I done this before?

Mother:　Even without coming to this direct confrontation you have come to understand the real situation and you have come to real creativity. This meeting brings to fruition the work that you have done. It is the icing on the cake. I am proud of you. You have done well. Thank you for carrying what I put on you unconsciously and still loving me. You, too, are a loving person.

Me:　You don't want me tied to you emotionally, do you?

Mother:　It keeps me back, as well as you.

Me:　How do we get disengaged?

Mother:　By talking like this, by facing the deep love and fear and anger we have for one another and loving each other for each other's growth.

Me:　How much of my compulsion is identification with you?

Mother:　It is more than this. Our relationship opened you to the archetypal world and its fascination, but your compulsions have a deeper root than personal relationship.

Me:　(*speaking to the Christ*) Lord, if I must bear these inner tensions I bear them as my cross. Help with the sacrifice.

Christ:　Be careful what you sacrifice. More growth and maturity will come, but growth is difficult and sometimes painful. Keep at it. But don't let Myra, your mother, stand there alone.

Me: Mother, Myra, friend, you kept me alive, but loused up my life. I have real ambivalence toward you, real love, real anger. . . .

Mother: I understand. I'm sorry I was so ignorant and confused and passed it on. The Evil One did a good job on me, too. I feel with you the pain you bear. I didn't face the split within me and it killed me. You have borne the pain. I am sorry for some of the inheritance I gave you, yet I love you and died for you—as did our Lord. . . .

[*I open my arms to her and we embrace. I feel her love and concern and I feel mine flowing out to her.*]

Me: I ask for your continued help and guidance from your perspective on the other side. Help me stay close to my Lord. I know you have continued with me and given me guidance after your death.

Mother: I love you and I have tried to make up for the damage that I have caused, to open doors and even give inspiration from time to time.

Me: Thank you for this time together. Thank you for your love and concern. Thank you so much for those words before you died, about your rejection of me as a child.

Mother: I love you, my son, my friend, my companion. Remember that there is a great difference between what I was, what I am now, and what your image of me was and is. Let us meet again. We are on the same path.

It is difficult to express the completion, peace, relief, and resolution this brought me. We are much more in touch with that other dimension than we sometimes realize. This is the essential meaning of the doctrine of the communion of saints included in the Apostles' Creed. Yet the church these days rarely suggests that we take this doctrine seriously. Thanks to Jung's advocacy of the active imagination, plus his understanding of the deceased as living on in reality, I was able to have this kind of meeting with my mother. It is difficult to tell in what sense this meeting was objective, but it seemed real to me.

Another use of the active imagination concerns conflicts with other people. For example, what can we do if we are having trouble with another person but fear that the other cannot listen to what we would like to say? We can use the same method with such a person as with the deceased. Then when the moment of face-to-face encounter arrives, most of the tensions will have been put aside. One knows what needs to be said and is able to say it. The imagination can open us to reconciliation, which is at the very heart of the Christian way. However, one must not use the imagination to try to influence others, but only to clarify the relationship.

Some people find it difficult to enter into the stream of the imagination, but may be able to write fairy tales, tell stories, or draw pictures. These methods reveal the depths of one's being almost as surely as dreams or active imagination, and can help us integrate and deal with unconscious material.

With the imagination, one can turn a mood into an image. Instead of avoiding the darkness and pain, I enter into it and try to visualize clearly what it is all about. Most of us flee from a mood that upsets us. We go to the movies, go running, play cards, or just try to forget it. An enormous amount of alcohol is consumed for the same purpose. Jung suggested that instead of fleeing from the mood, we turn toward it and try to enter into it, try to discover what it is saying to us. If we leave it in darkness we can destroy ourselves. We need to enter it and stay with it until we find light. This takes courage and persistence. Again we need to be like that importunate widow who kept after the judge until she received justice.

Jesus teaches us to keep at our task. We have to make a decision for light, love, and Christ. *Life does not bring one inevitably toward light.* Without our conscious decision to move toward light and love, our road usually ends in the pit. This truth is described in the story of the fall of Adam and Eve, and in the doctrine of original sin. Something within us needs to seek for light and love. Therefore, when I enter into a mood, I am going to stick with it until I find a light. That is the meaning of the cross. Jesus knew how to stick it through until he found resurrection. He gives this hope to every one of us. I could not say this except as a Christian. This conviction is rare among Jungians. Existentialists, like Camus and Sartre, do not persist through and so leave us in darkness and in the pit.

The following dialogue was written as I was riding in the car on my way to give some lectures in Michigan. Barbara was driving. I felt terrible and wondered how I could give the lectures in such a mood. I wrote out the experiences as we drove along:

Me: The darkness is tugging at me from the center; the lead ball is hanging from the depth of me, inner weariness, inner hopelessness.

Dark Voice: All is hopeless, all vain. Curl up and die.

Me: You have me in your grasp again so that a large part of me would like to give up. You are very seductive. You speak within and make me think that I am speaking. The deadly poppies lure me to sleep and death. There is a murmuring within: "Go to sleep and die."

Dark Voice: There is no meaning or value. All is lost and vain, hopeless. There is only matter, no purpose, all vain, creep into thy narrow bed, creep, let no more be said. Strew on her roses, roses, in quiet she reposes, ah, would that I did, too. . . .

Me: The siren voice calls me. The task seems so hard, life so difficult, so futile, the darkness attractive, the endless rest is not me but the darkness being seductive, destructive and seductive, and speaking from within. . . .

Dark Voice: Give up and sleep, pull the plug. . . .

Me: What, Lord, do I do?

Voice: Go with it and see where it leads you.

[*I enter the silence and see and follow a beautiful young buxom woman into the poppy field. She dances ahead of me. As I go on I realize that the fumes of the poppies are overwhelming me, but I go on and the sweet fumes overpower me and I collapse. As I fall I see a mask fall from the woman's face and I see that behind the mask is a death's head. I fall to the ground, but I do not lose consciousness. Rather my consciousness is separated from my body and I watch my body from outside. Elves emerge from a hole in the ground near my body. The deadly woman points to my body. They laugh with glee and come dancing around the body, which lies there amid the poppies. They rip off my clothes and jab the body with knife-sharp sticks and pitchforks. I am separated from it, yet I must stay with it; and I can faintly feel that they are doing all this to me. They perpetrate every vileness upon this body of mine. I wonder why they want to do this. Their jabs reach to the heart of the body. Then they hack up the body into little pieces and then carry the pieces of it back into their underground place. There it will rot and they will feed it to the soil. The woman has adjusted her mask and has gone out to lure other unsuspecting travelers into the field of poppies with her plaintive song.*]

Me: Lord, I have followed it through. Here I am, lost and fragmented, my spirit cut off from my rotting body. What now? How can this be redeemed? Why the pain again and again?

Inner Voice: Your busyness has opened you to the destructive and seductive voices once again. You have tried to save the whole world and have lost yourself. In turning your mood into an image you have simply allowed your self to realize consciously what has already happened unconsciously. This is why the inner pain and darkness must be faced through. It has already happened. The mood of darkness is the reflection of an inner event that has already taken place. The seduction took place over these last weeks when you thought that you could do more than a human being. Until you stepped into that mood and realized the reality of what had already taken place within you, I could not turn it around for you. The imagination brings you to the reality of your inner being, to what is actually there, to what has already taken place. I can only change reality when it is acknowledged.

Me: Lord, this is where I am, torn, broken, fragmented. Help! Help! [*There is a blinding light, a lightning strike, a crash of thunder. the earth hears and trembles and spits out the pieces of me, rotten, stinking, like excrement.*]

Me: And what can you do with these rotting fragments?

Inner Voice: Quiet, child, I made you and I can remake you.

[*He takes the pieces in his hand and it is like a million spiders weaving webs. Out of the rotting fragments emerges a body, a better body than before. He calls to me.*]

Inner Voice: Come, child, inhabit this body again and be whole.

[*As He holds that body of mine, I return so that I can feel His loving embrace, the embrace of the creator, lover, transformer, redeemer. I realize that He has carried me again to the pool that lies at the foot of the cliff, from which the spring flows. The sun is sinking and I rest and sleep. He holds me close until morning when I awake and am alive again. Here is the perfectly whole one, union of opposites. We laugh and play. We come down to the sea and the white sand. Naked we play in the warm waves, and they renew me more and more. Then we walk up along the beach to a cottage that stands on the rocks above the ocean. The sun is setting as He leads me up to it. A cool wind comes up*] *from the sea. He gives me a tunic of lambskins and lights a fire on the hearth. We laugh and talk.*]

Me: Even though I am a lecherous and egocentric fool, do You still love me, Lord? I do not understand why you continue to care and help me when I call. I am not worthy.

Inner Voice: Child, who is to say how worthy anything is, but Me? I know your condition. I loved Peter, who denied me, and Paul, who persecuted me. You are trying and you live close to the abyss. You have grown much. Keep trying. My love is forever. Rest in My love. Speak it forth.

Me: I'll try. Please Lord, pick me up again when I fall. Continue with me.[2]

NOTES

1. C. G. Jung: *Analytical Psychology: Its Theory and Practice* (New York: Random House, 1970), pp. 192 ff.

2. Several of these dialogues are found in my book *Adventure Inward* (Minneapolis: Augsburg, 1980).

EPILOGUE

At the Last Supper, knowing the fate that awaited him, Jesus rose, put his garments aside, wrapped a towel around himself, poured water into a basin, and began to wash the feet of the disciples.

What do we say to Jesus Christ when he comes to wash our feet?

When Jesus came to Peter, the disciple exclaimed, "Lord, are you going to wash my feet?" Jesus answered, "You do not know what I am doing. Later you will know." But Peter said to him, "You will never wash my feet." Jesus responded, "If I do not wash your feet, you will no longer be my disciple." Peter cried out then, "Lord, do not wash only my feet then, but wash my hands and my head also." Jesus said, "Whoever has taken a bath is perfectly clean and does not need to be washed, except for his feet."

After he washed the feet of all the disciples, he returned to the table, put on his garments and said, "Do you understand what I have done for you? You call me Teacher and Lord. It is fitting that you call me thus, for I am your Teacher and Lord. As I have just washed your feet, you should then wash one another's feet. I have given an example for you. As I have done, so you should do. I give you a new commandment. Love one another as I have loved you. So you must love one another. If you have love for one another, then all will know that you are my disciples."

Jesus already knew that Judas would betray him, that Peter would deny him. Yet he washed the feet of all his disciples, forgiving them in advance their trespasses. He knew their weaknessess, their vulnerability to the Evil One.

Jung gave us a way to know the world and ourselves. We can accept his gifts with gratitude, humility, and the will to use them to overcome confusion and find the purpose of our lives. Jung gave us a way to penetrate the spiritual world and receive the treasures that the risen Christ is waiting to bestow on us. We thank the Lord of life for the help of his servant Jung in giving us the "how." Jung points our attention to the depth and truth of Christianity. Although reluctant at first, Jung went into the vineyard. The grapes he picked can be used for the wine of the Eucharist.